CATCHING
LEADERSHIP

The Art of Letting Go and Hooking into Leadership
Through *C.A.T.C.H. & Release*®

MICHAEL LEYTEM

Catching Leadership
The Art of Letting Go and Hooking into Leadership
Through *C.A.T.C.H. & Release*®

Print Edition: March 2020
Copyright ©2020 Michael Leytem, LLC
ISBN: 9781677875948
Published in the USA

Illustrations: Wes Leytem
Graphic Design: Austin Marshall

Michael Leytem, LLC Publishing
8333 Foothill Blvd.
Rancho Cucamonga, California 91730
www.catchingleadership.com

To personalize your journey through this book, I highly recommend you take a moment to visit www.catchingleadership.com and take the C.A.T.C.H. & Release Leadership Index (CARLI). The CARLI provides valuable insights on your strengths and development areas as they pertain to each section of the C.A.T.C.H. & Release Model. The items used in the CARLI have been reviewed and vetted by subject matter experts and a pilot of the instrument has yielded highly reliable results. Please note that the CARLI was created solely to be used as a tool to guide development. This instrument was not designed to aid in the hiring/firing of employees or influence merit-based decisions. To learn more about the CARLI and other Catching Leadership resources, please visit www.catchingleadership.com.

Dedicated to my wife Alisha,
the person who believed in me
before I believed in myself

Table of Contents

Introduction

*"Many men go fishing all of their lives without knowing
that it is not fish they are after."*
-Henry David Thoreau

At the bottom of Lake St. Clair there is a rock pile that serves as a sanctuary to a fish that still haunts me. The fish doesn't have a name, although *Regret, Embarrassment,* and *Shame* would all suffice. I have no desire to embellish this story like other fishing stories you may have heard. Truth be told the fish was probably 2-3 lbs. and maybe 18 inches on a good day. A healthy smallmouth bass nonetheless, but definitely no giant. The great tragedy of this story is that on that cold and windy fall day, nearly a decade ago, I was never able to make the proper introduction with my aquatic friend. Even worse, the bite was slower than slow and it was the Big Ten Classic where I was representing the University of Iowa Bass Fishing Team. For all I knew, that one fish could have made the difference between a top three and bottom three finish. Given the unique circumstances of Mother Nature that day, our team had to try some new techniques, many of which I was not familiar with. I had just one bite the entire day and like most bites in life, it came unexpectedly. Alas, that fish never made it into our livewell. As my teammate tried to net my catch, fate showed its ugly face again, allowing the fish to unhook itself just a couple of feet from the side of the boat. The agony that festered inside of me watching that fish swim back down to its rockpile took years to evaporate. I missed a golden opportunity to help our team on that day, but over time I've used it to catch something much greater.

By opening this book you have decided to fish for leadership in an entirely new way. A way that will strengthen and expand the leadership net you cast today and for many years to come. Knot by knot, I will teach you how to tie together the most important elements of leadership, psychology, and mindfulness to foster meaningful growth. If you are not a fishing fanatic fear not, this is a leadership book first and foremost, not a fishing book. All readers, whether currently leading or aspiring to one day, will have something to gain by understanding the concepts laid out in this book. My main goal is to help you *C.A.T.C.H. & Release* whatever it is holding you back from being the leader you were meant to be.

Regardless of where you are today on your leadership journey, there is a reason you have picked up this book. Perhaps to learn something new about yourself, or because someone you admire recommended it? Maybe you felt bad for the author attempting to spin his passion for fishing as leadership, or maybe your intention is to criticize it. Either way, all are welcome. My intention for this book is to have a positive impact on anyone allowing it to. As your captain, I promise to steer you in the right direction, but the heavy lifting will be up to you. I can assure you this: if you are honest with yourself, willing to explore new tactics and keep an open mind, you will receive the greatest gift there is, an opportunity to grow.

So why fishing? Well, here's a fun fact you may not know: fishing is a hobby enjoyed by over 49 million Americans every year. It ranks only behind running activities as the most popular outdoor recreational activity people participate in, and, surprisingly 60% of anglers (a.k.a. fishermen) are under the age of 45 (Recreational Fishing - Statistics & Facts, 2017). What is it about fishing that hooks so many anglers to the sport each year? Is it the peaceful environment and mental stillness nature offers? Is it the ongoing puzzle of trying to figure out where and what exactly the fish are biting on today? Or is it something deeper that resides inside the mindset of the angler brought more to life with every sunset and sunrise? Perhaps the real mystique of fishing is visualizing the unseen world which exists just below the surface. Whatever it may be, the one certainty in fishing is uncertainty. Just as in life, changes to fishing patterns happen rapidly. Minute by minute, month by month, year by year, unique circumstances contribute to a changing environment. It's for this very reason that many people cherish the memories they make on the water so much. The sport offers an escape into a physical and mental place that allows us to connect with something primitive yet present. Somewhere nestled in the consistent inconsistencies, people are able to release whatever baggage they once held onto while simultaneously absorbing nature's unrelenting beauty.

Even for the most novice of anglers, fishing offers the perfect setting to explore life beyond the surface and into new depths of enlightenment. Of course, fishing provides an opportunity to catch fish, but as Thoreau alluded to, it's often not fish most anglers are after. I believe that there is something else to be caught, deep within ourselves, which, when applied correctly, has the ability to create a legacy of leading others.

As a leadership consultant and coach, there is a fascinating, yet simple question I enjoy asking people of all walks of life: *What makes a great leader?* The variety of responses I receive is quite entertaining. I'm sure you can guess some of the most common answers I hear. A leader is someone who is... (fill in the blank) *strong, confident, caring, well-spoken, doesn't care what others think, has great hair, etc.* Okay, so maybe I made up the last one about the hair, but you get the point. Every time I ask the question, there are usually a fair number of typical responses; however, what I find more fascinating than the common responses are the vague responses. A leader is someone who is... *you know... who just has it.* Which is usually followed by me asking *could you be a little more specific?* To which the reply is often *YOU know... they just get it.* Although I try my best to understand what people are really saying when they tell me a leader just has *it* (whatever *it* really is), I'm never entirely sure. For the longest time, I attributed these vague responses to one of two conclusions: 1.) A way to encompass the entire spectrum of leadership characteristics in one simple two-letter word, or, 2.) A dichotomy for people to reinforce the idea that leadership is a trait that people either have or do not have. Until recently, I've come to a new conclusion.

Perhaps the reason so many people describe leadership as *it* is due to the changing environments which leaders now find themselves in. You would agree that the perception of a leader today looks much different than it did a century ago, right? How about a decade ago or even a presidential cycle ago? Perhaps *it* is a reflection of the changing times, the current leaders we surround ourselves with, and the evolving requirements that make leaders effective in today's day and age. After all, if the mental schemas we have created for leadership have changed, so too will our perceptions and ultimately the way we describe *it*.

As challenging as it can be, the speed at which the world is changing offers us a brand new opportunity to reexamine what we think effective leadership is today, and I'm not sure that question gets asked enough. It may surprise you, but in this age of Netflix, many organizations still choose to operate with the same mindset they did back when getting a new release from Blockbuster made them feel special. Although the days of VHS and cassette tapes are long gone, ineffective leadership behaviors from decades ago still live on. No more are the days that all the answers are held by one person at the top. Thus, the ability to remain open to new ideas, make agile decisions based on changing information, and rely on other people and systems to provide expertise has become imperative for a leader's success.

Consider this same point through the lens of communication—a key ingredient of success for anything in life. Modes of communication have evolved so rapidity in recent years that many leaders are at a loss deciding which method is appropriate, effective, and compatible with their latest mobile update. As texting competes for the preferred method of communication over face-to-face interactions, we find ourselves in truly different times. But, with all change comes opportunity, and with opportunity comes a decision. Leaders today have to decide: *Embrace the changing world we now live in or slowly become obsolete.* The fight between change and stability is over; change delivered a knockout punch in the first round and shows no sign of slowing down. As change continues to disrupt the world as we know it, leadership will become increasingly important in navigating shifts in people, processes, and technology, not to mention the generational elephant in the room.

With baby boomers departing rapidly from the leadership party and millennials making their grand entrance, who is going to chaperone? The current dynamic of the workforce in terms of generational differences creates a whole new level of challenge for leaders at every level. Given that there is no way to possibly comprehend the pressures each generation experienced in their upbringing, leaders have to do their best to understand multiple perspectives and respect each generation in the workplace, regardless of age or stereotypes. One thing everyone can agree on is the rapid rate of technological advances each subsequent generation grew up with. Take a second to think about how drastically phone communication has changed for recent generations. From group landlines to single landlines, from payphones to car phones, from caller id to pagers, from Nokia cell phones to flip phones to smartphones, and smartphones to smart accessories—it's easy to see how technology and modes of communication have dramatically shaped generational experiences. Nearly every aspect of life (work, dating, shopping, etc.) has been significantly impacted by the transformation of the phone in the last few decades. None of this is a surprise to you, but the point is that rapid technological changes can make generations feel even further apart from the actual number of years between them. In the age of hashtags, memes, and GIFs, we all need to challenge the labels we hold for different generations. With technology showing no signs of slowing the generational divide, leaders will be needed to help close the gap.

As easy as it is to recognize the differences between generations, it is much more important for leaders to emphasize the common elements they share. People from all generations face challenges, are required to adapt, and want to make a meaningful difference in the world. Great leaders understand this, that's why they don't build walls between generations, they build bridges to connect them. Possessing an attitude of *kids today just don't understand the way it was for us,* or on the flip side, *old people are so stuck in their ways,* doesn't foster collaboration from either side. Effective leaders fully understand the political and cultural environment they work in and find ways to gain commitment across different groups. As a leader, you will need to continue to acknowledge, accept, and find new ways to embrace diversity whether from generational differences or from the realm of all other differences that make humanity so unique.

No leader has the power to stop time, and time will undoubtedly continue to transform some aspects of leadership, but not all. One of my favorite artists, Bob Marley, sang it best, *"In this bright future, you can't forget your past."* (Ford, 1974). To fully understand and appreciate where humanity is going, we must learn from the leadership lessons of our past. The concept of leadership development has been part of the human experience from the onset. Survival, for our ancestors, required tremendous amounts of leadership and a willingness to grow in order for our gene pool to continue on. While the mental schemes of leadership look very different today, there are still many aspects of leadership that have stood and will continue to stand the test of time. Ancient texts are filled with accounts of leaders needing to persevere through adversity, make unprecedented decisions, and form strategic relationships in order to achieve results. Leadership constructs such as courage, collaboration, and adaptability were staples then just as they are today, even if the landscape (i.e. cave to skyscraper) has drastically changed where leaders operate from. Even amid all the changes we are experiencing today, there is no need to reinvent the leadership wheel. There is, however, an opportunity to add the engine, seats, and power steering to equip leaders with the vehicle needed for tomorrow's success. Just as fishing was still fishing in ancient times, leadership is still leadership today, but a need exists to upgrade the tools and techniques in order to maximize its effectiveness.

The Evolution of Catching Leadership

As constructs of leadership past, present, and future continue to mold the way leadership is portrayed, I strongly feel that as a society we have missed the mark on emphasizing what it is that truly makes a great leader. There seems to be a strong tendency to equate leadership to the number of achievements an individual possesses, how much money they make, or even how big their social media following is. Merely focusing on individual achievements as a leader only paints a small piece of the picture. The question not asked often enough is how many other great leaders has a leader developed throughout their career and what was the collective impact of those leaders? A legacy of leadership is not only marked by personal accolades, but also by the rippling impact a leader has on others. The most successful leaders are the ones who can set aside their personal egos and fully develop other leaders to grow beyond even their own capabilities. Think about some of the greatest leaders you have come to know in your lifetime. Chances are those leaders took the time to openly share their knowledge and skills with you (and others) to make a positive impact on your development. Now, think of some of the worst leaders you have come to know. Chances are those leaders cared less about making an impact on others and more about personal gain or looking good in front of others. Leadership has always been about *"we,"* but far too often our need for recognition has made it about *"me."* As you continue to develop your own leadership skills, it is crucial that you also identify future leaders along the way and develop those aspiring individuals without feeling threatened or jealous of their achievements.

The most rewarding work you will ever experience as a leader comes in the form of developing others.

Expanding on this concept in the context of fishing, I want you to think of leaders who measure their success solely based on the number of trophy fish they mount (i.e. personal achievement). These individuals prefer to fish alone, hoard their secrets, and lust for opportunities to receive recognition. When the moment arises, and these leaders successfully land a trophy fish, they find no one there to celebrate with them. What then do these leaders do? Likely, they hurry back to the marina to start bragging to anyone they can find about how great they are. Myopic leaders behave this way because they are trying to fill a void. They seek validation and approval from others because they are unable to break from their own limiting beliefs (e.g. *if I share my knowledge and train someone else they might be better than me*). If they were able to behave more transparently and create mutually beneficial experiences, they wouldn't need to seek the limelight to feel better about themselves when fishing alone. Unfortunately, these leaders miss out on the internal satisfaction that comes with developing others in an authentic and non-threatening way. There is no trophy that proves a leader's success like the one their apprentice holds up. Keep in mind that a mounted fish is just a mounted fish unless others are willing to carry on the legend of the *C.A.T.C.H.*

How People Fish Tell You How They Lead

It goes without saying that leaders today experience tremendous amounts of pressure to deliver in a complex and ever-changing environment. With all of the time, energy, and devotion that goes into leading oneself and others, it is crucial that leaders learn how to *Release*. Finding effective ways to self-reflect, let go of limiting beliefs, and experience gratitude throughout the process is what makes the journey worthwhile. Tell me, what's the point of wanting to lead if all you experience is constant stress, feelings of inadequacy, and negativity? Who would want to sign up for that?

Throughout the years, I've noticed that many popular leadership development models fail to emphasize the importance of the *Release*. Ironically, we hear stories all the time of successful leaders who prioritize time to take care of themselves—mind, body, and soul, yet this part of the equation is often missing from leadership textbooks. The formula for longevity as a leader is finding balance throughout the journey. Learning how to effectively self-reflect, release negativity, and stay mindful throughout the process will benefit you greatly. As a leader, your thoughts paint your reality and what you focus on grows. Being intentional in how you speak about yourself, the way you want to feel, and what you ultimately want to achieve starts and ends with your mindset. It's time for leaders all over the world to start harnessing the power of the *Release*.

Practicing what I preach, I have been spending a lot of time thinking about what the changing landscape of leadership means for my own development. I find myself asking questions about whether or not I am making the right choices in my life to develop into the man I want to be. How will I know when I am on the right path? Am I learning everything I need to know to be successful? What are the gaps I need to fill to make me a great leader? Maybe these questions sound familiar to the types of questions you've been asking about yourself. Have you recognized a pattern of behaviors you demonstrate when thoughts of uncertainty and doubt come up? How do you find peace? Where do you go to reflect?

During times of deep reflection, I find myself desiring to be outdoors. Nature has a way of clearing my thoughts, which provides me a chance to breathe and realign myself. As a result, I have made strong mental connections between nature and my own mental clarity. Every time I reconnect with nature, I always find myself leaving with greater insight and a lighter feeling than I had prior.

It dawned on me one day that this personal connection to nature was more nuanced than just being outdoors. When I took a minute to reflect on all of the major lessons and milestones in my life, a recurring theme continued to emerge: fishing. Fishing was and continues to be, my north star for major life events and personal development. From the time I was just a young child learning the basics from my father, to the cherished memories I made with elementary friends on the Mississippi River, to the lifelong buddies I made on the University of Iowa Bass Fishing Team, to catching a fish on my wedding day (that actually happened), and finally landing a giant bass the day I decided to write this book, fishing has always been a cornerstone in my life. It helped me bond with grad school professors, secure my first consulting job, and today has given me the courage to launch my own business. But what exactly is it about fishing that has led me to good fortune?

In many cultures, fishing is viewed as a symbol of good luck and prosperity, but I believe there is something far more valuable than just that. Fishing isn't about throwing a line into the water and waiting to get lucky, it's an incredibly rewarding yet mentally challenging experience, just like leadership development. After every cast, every catch, and even every miss, there are valuable lessons to be learned contributing to the mastery of the art. The second you think you have it all figured out is the second you are humbly reminded that you still have so much to learn.

Realizing the parallels of two great passions of mine and the growing need for leadership development in the digital age inspired me to develop the *C.A.T.C.H. & Release* Model of Leadership. The goal of this model is to serve as a guide for you on your journey to create a lasting legacy of leadership.

Having spent several years as a consultant in the leadership development and talent management space, it became apparent to me that a lot of the tools and methods used to develop leadership are limited in their scope and point of view. Many of the most widely-used assessments are several decades old and were created during a time that the environment in which leaders were navigating was much different. Think about it for a second. Would it make much sense for a surgeon to use a textbook from the 1970s to prepare for surgery with the tools and technology we have today? So why would it make any more sense for us to use outdated tools and techniques to develop our future leaders? I am not suggesting that we throw everything out, but rather that we modify the recipe with new ingredients that fulfill the appetite for what hungry leaders need today.

Taking a holistic view, I examined and documented the key constructs that I observed while working with hundreds of leaders in Fortune 500 companies over the last decade. I particularly paid close attention to the constructs that differentiated good leaders from great leaders. Considering multiple perspectives, the social psychology, and mental processes that promote long-term growth and fulfillment, I created a unique journey to help those willing to develop their leadership skills and leave behind a legacy they can feel proud of. Using this framework, anyone who possesses a drive to develop and a willingness to be honest with themselves will find new ways to realize their leadership potential.

Each chapter in this book represents one part of the *C.A.T.C.H. & Release* Model, which is depicted in the graphic below.

The *C.A.T.C.H. & Release* Model

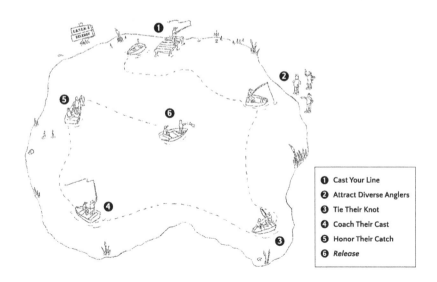

1. Cast Your Line
2. Attract Diverse Anglers
3. Tie Their Knot
4. Coach Their Cast
5. Honor Their Catch
6. *Release*

While each step described in the *C.A.T.C.H. & Release* Model builds upon the prior, the individual constructs within each chapter do not require you to read them in any particular order. It's perfectly acceptable to skim and scan various sections or even entire chapters of this book. Additionally, you may find yourself having to put the book down from time to time in order to process what a particular leadership construct means to you. I encourage you to do just that—grab a journal and pause often to reflect and document the learnings and ideas you discover throughout your journey. Leadership is not a race, consume what you need when you need to. My goal is for you to find, in your own time, whatever it is you need to grow into the best leader you can be. While there is certainly greater value in reading this book from start to finish, please use the information provided in a way that best suits you, and remember to grab that journal, it will serve you well.

Before we embark on this journey, I want to ask you a powerful, yet incredibly simple, question: Why do you want to lead? Take a moment, set down this book if you have to, and answer that question. If you don't know, seriously, put the book down. Close your eyes, take a deep breath and think about it. It might take you a minute, but gaining clarity on this will be paramount to your future growth.

Fully understanding your honest motivation to lead is imperative to your long-term success. If you can't answer the question above in a simple and concise way at the moment, that's OK. Very few people can. A great place to start is by creating a leadership statement. A leadership statement is a customized vision that will guide you in the decisions you make as a leader and serve as a simple reminder to why you have decided to take on the challenge of becoming a leader in the first place. Through the rough waters and dark clouds you will face on this journey, your leadership statement will always serve as your anchor.

To develop a leadership statement, grab a piece of paper (or your journal) and follow these 4 simple steps:

1. Write down three core values that you hold with the highest regard

2. Write down three strengths you possess
3. Write down the specific group(s) of people you seek to lead
4. Write down a specific goal you would like to achieve with the specific group listed above

Now fill in the blanks for the following statement:

As a leader who values (core value 1, core value 2, and core value 3,) I pledge to use my strengths of (strength 1, strength 2, strength 3,) to help (a specific group of people) (achieve a specific goal.)

Here is an example:

As a leader who values *kindness, diversity,* and *vulnerability,* I pledge to use my strengths of *writing, coaching,* and *learning from my failures* to help *my readers become better equipped with the knowledge and tools needed to successfully lead in the digital age.*

By completing your leadership statement, you now have your *why.* Keep this statement in mind when you begin to doubt yourself. Remember that you have important values to guide you, strengths to give to the world, and a group of people who need your leadership as they try to achieve a meaningful goal.

As we begin this journey, I want to tell you that I applaud your open-mindedness to view leadership through a new lens. I am inspired by your determination to continue your own development and am truly grateful to be your captain on this journey. Although the path to building a legacy of great leadership does not come easy, know that my intentions for creating this new model come from a place of encouragement, enlightenment, and acceptance. Now let's begin.

*To personalize your journey through this book, I highly recommend you visit www.catchingleadership.com and take the C.A.T.C.H. & Release Leadership Index (CARLI). The CARLI provides valuable insights on your strengths and development areas as they pertain to each section of the C.A.T.C.H. & Release Model. The items used in the CARLI have been reviewed and vetted by subject matter experts and a pilot of the instrument has yielded highly reliable results. To learn more about the CARLI and other Catching Leadership resources, please visit www.catchingleadership.com.

CHAPTER 1:

Cast Your Line

Understand Your Skill Set and Lead by Example

"Be the change you wish to see in the world."

-MAHATMA GANDHI

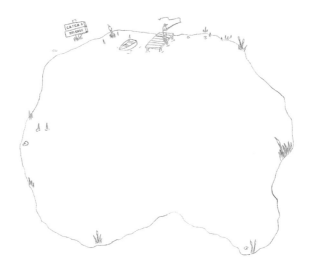

Leadership Constructs Discussed in *Cast Your Line*

Adaptability • Emotional Intelligence • Authenticity
Continuous Improvement • Perseverance
Inspirational Influence • Clear Communication
Courage • Decision Making • Integrity
Drive for Results • Effective Delegation

Dead stick fishing was a novelty to me that day on Lake St. Clair. With strong winds, no cover, and the tournament on the line, I had no choice but to learn as quickly as possible how to properly dead stick a 4-inch green pumpkin tube to catch the smallmouth bass we needed to stay competitive in the tournament. The name of the game was patience and extreme stillness. We cast our tubes over rock piles and stood motionless, letting the wind push the boat at a few mph causing the tube to drag across the bottom of the translucent lake like an injured crayfish. Spending hours on the water, trying to stay warm, and keep our spirits high, I thought to myself: *This must be the dumbest kind of fishing there is, why would anyone on Earth want to dead stick for smallies?* I had no desire to master this technique, in fact, I didn't even really believe it would work. All I wanted to do was go cast a spinnerbait or Texas-rigged creature bait in the shallows because that's what I was comfortable with, that's where my skill set was the strongest.

Developing yourself as a leader begins and ends with you. You are the one who accepts the responsibility to lead. You are the one who seeks the truth about who you are and who you want to be. You are the individual who sets the goals, determines the pace, and is held accountable to follow through on your commitments. You are the leader who needs to *Cast Your Line* first before teaching others how to do the same.

Flip it, pitch it, skip it, overhand it, sidearm it, vertical jig it, slow-roll it, dead stick it, troll it, or even noodle it. The right cast at the right time will greatly determine how successful you are as an angler unless you are noodling, then you are just crazy (look up noodling if you don't know what it is). Whether you know the techniques listed above, or it sounds like complete gibberish, the point is still the same—there are many ways to fish, just as there are many ways to lead.

Accurately understanding your skill set is vital to your effectiveness as a leader; however, the mere comprehension of your skills is not enough. You must be willing to put your skills into practice and lead by example. This will be especially true for new skills you learn along the way, or in my case—the art of dead sticking. The tendency for people to avoid what they don't know is also true in leadership. Unfamiliarity makes people feel vulnerable, and being vulnerable can lead to thoughts of inadequacy or incompetence. The pattern of rejecting new knowledge or learning new skills is initially rewarding—or at least your brain thinks so—because it can protect you from possible humiliation and discomfort. Unfortunately, this short-term defense mechanism often ends up causing more pain and hardships down the road surfacing at the most inconvenient times.

Casting Across a Variety of Leadership Situations

Through the lens of fishing, imagine coming up to what appears to be the perfect spot (i.e. an area with thick cover, protected from the wind, and at the exact depth the fish have been biting at). As you slowly pull closer you notice several tree branches decorated with lures from past anglers' unsuccessful attempts. If you currently do not possess the skills needed to make the cast, you may be wishing you had spent more time practicing prior to this opportunity. You may even recall a time you planned to learn a new cast but procrastinated your development due to other competing priorities. You now find yourself in a predicament on how to properly place your lure in the strike zone. Part of you may be telling yourself: Look, everyone else tried and failed here, why would it be any different for me? While another part of you knows, that the best results in life come from a willingness to try new approaches and learn from failures. Regardless of whether you try to cast in this spot or not, you make a mental note never to be caught in this same predicament in the future. You promise never to feel ill-prepared again by not having the right skill(s) for the situation. Leadership opportunities are no different. They will continue to challenge you in new ways and require you to make an ongoing effort to better understand your current abilities and continuously develop new ones along the way. If neglected, the same challenges will continue to expose your blind spots time and time again.

Before we walk, we crawl, and before we catch, we cast. The first step of the *C.A.T.C.H. & Release* Model requires you to focus on your own foundational leadership skills before you are able to effectively develop others. Accurately understanding your current strengths and development areas is paramount to your success as a leader—the key-word, though, is *accurately*. Chances are you think you know what you are good at and what still needs work. Perhaps you have reinforced certain labels given to you throughout your life. Some may be true; some maybe not so true. Remember that every person on the planet regardless of title, income, or background has the capacity to demonstrate leadership. While the exact skills and proficiencies may vary from person to person, the opportunity to be a leader is universal.

I want you to reflect on three questions (grab your journal if it's handy):

> 1.) *Of all the skills I possess, which ones make me unique as a leader?*

2.) Which strengths can I leverage even more than I already do today?

3.) Which development areas present the greatest gaps in my ability to lead in the future?

Answering these questions in an honest manner will help you as you examine each construct within this chapter. Remember that every leader is unique because no two leaders possess exactly the same skill set. Knowing this, I want you to deeply reflect on what it is you bring to the table today. Critically think about all the skills you possess and how the unique combination of each makes up your own DNA as a leader.

If you haven't done so already, I encourage you to take the *C.A.T.C.H. & Release* Leadership Index (CARLI) at www.catchingleadership.com. The results will provide you with new insights to help you answer the questions above. If you have already taken the assessment, perhaps now would be a good time to journal on some of your key takeaways from the assessment. As needed, periodically refer to the glossary at the end of this book to reflect on the subconstructs that make up each dimension of the *C.A.T.C.H. & Release* Model.

Being the best leader you can be is not about playing a part or fitting a specific mold. There is no one size fits all or magic pill you can take to wake up one day as a great leader. Efforts to force a particular style of leadership on someone where no organic alignment exists is futile. Take this moment to quiet the noise and stereotypes of what you think leadership is. At its core, leadership is about harnessing the power of your uniqueness. Once you truly believe that leadership is a personal journey, you will be able to become more honest with yourself, resulting in greater acceptance and a stronger desire to grow.

In its purest form, leadership is about discovery. Discovering the abilities, drivers, and potential within yourself. Trying to emulate someone or something you have no desire to become only creates a barrier to realizing your true potential. This barrier ripples beyond even yourself—it ripples onto the development of others and can negatively impact your own fulfillment in life. If you aren't true to yourself as a leader, how can you ever expect others to act in a way that is true to themselves? If you desire to build your own legacy of leadership, you need to own your truth and embrace your uniqueness. Beyond your own understanding, you will also need to encourage others to discover their own individual values, skills, and tendencies that make them, them. We will take a deeper dive into understanding others in the chapters to come, but before we get ahead of ourselves, let's focus on learning how to cast your own line. Remember, every *C.A.T.C.H.* first starts with a cast.

The decision to pick up the rod and reel for the first time can be just as intimidating as your first leadership experience. The initial fear of failure or concerns about looking foolish can paralyze people before they even start. The novelty of any new experience typically produces more doubt than optimism. Thoughts of embarrassment or vulnerability lead some people to play it safe rather than trying to learn how to cast into new waters. It's much easier to succeed at things we already know, but if we aren't catching the type of experiences we need to grow, what's the point of casting a line in the first place?

Opening yourself up to casting in new ways will always produce a chance of initial failure. In order to maximize success and reduce the risk of unintentional harm, it's your job to be aware of your surroundings and accurately understand the equipment (i.e. skill set) you possess. Regardless of your current leadership level, there will always be new experiences that will mirror the first time you picked up a rod and reel. Owning and understanding your unique strengths and development areas will allow you to learn new casts, which can be applied across all leadership situations, new and old.

In both fishing and leadership, there is a tendency for people to glorify success and make judgments solely based on outward appearances. This pitfall can lead some to think that leaders are just lucky or *born that way.* However, when looking below the surface (i.e. the fancy cars, expensive gadgets, and custom-tailored attire), one can quickly see that, like anything, improving leadership comes down to the basic principles of practice and self-discipline. Every expert in a field, or master of a craft, typically spends countless hours honing their skills and improving themselves. As easy as it may be to accredit success to luck, luck typically has little to do with it.

Luck Has Little To Do With Leadership

To illustrate this point further I want to step outside of the realm of fishing for a moment and into the realm of music. As someone who grew up playing guitar, I often used to wonder how some of the most famous musicians became pros. One of my favorite guitarists, and perhaps the greatest of all time, was Jimi Hendrix. As a teenager, I kept asking myself how did Jimi get so good? *Was he just lucky or born that way?* Given that I had spent numerous hours with calloused fingers trying to learn a couple of basic chords, my initial inclination was to believe Jimi was just a freak of nature, born with the inherent gift to shred. Not having the luxury to see his work ethic, ingenuity, and perseverance first hand, it was easier for me to conclude that he came out of the womb with a guitar in his hand lighting up the fretboard in mind-blowing fashion. Now honestly ask yourself this, when you see a clip of a legend like Jimi performing an unprecedented act, what is your first thought? Likely it's not about all of the failures, learnings, and countless hours of practice that went into learning that skill. Chances are you probably think to yourself: *It must be nice to be born with that kind of talent*, followed by some thought of comparison like, *Why wasn't I lucky enough to be born with a skill like that?* We will uncover the downsides of comparisons in a later chapter, but for now, let's examine what made Jimi truly special.

The truth is Jimi practiced like a madman. He often spent up to ten hours a day experimenting with new techniques and tones on his guitar. His path to greatness was not one that was paved for him with a silver spoon in his mouth. From a young age, he traveled, took risks, and made adjustments early in his career, which ultimately led him to one of his biggest breaks—headlining Woodstock in 1969. Some mornings it was said that Jimi would grab his guitar before even putting his pants on. Regardless of Jimi's preferred attire, the point is that people often don't see the grind that goes into development—instead, they tend to focus on the outcomes, outer appearance, or luck.

These blinders, blocking the less attractive reality of the grind, are further accentuated through social media. When was the last time you saw a post about a friend not receiving a promotion? Not getting that job or falling short of that weight loss goal they set for themselves last month? So often, when we see others' successes on social media, we attribute that success to luck, since we are not privy to the journey leading up to that outcome. This same logic often gets applied to success in fishing. Attributing catching fish to pure luck may be the simplest explanation for us to understand, but it fails to tell the whole story. The kind of fishing and leadership development I promote does not require luck, but it does require a great deal of practice and self-discipline.

THE 12 CASTING TECHNIQUES OF LEADERSHIP

So, if everyone can agree that practice is key, where does one start? To help you focus on what I have observed as the most meaningful fundamentals of leadership, I have outlined *The 12 Casting Techniques of Leadership*. Think of each type of cast as a unique leadership concept that can improve your overall effectiveness to lead. Keep in mind, just as every leadership skill is not appropriate for every leadership situation, every casting technique is not appropriate for every fishing situation. While leveraging a *skipping cast* may be extremely effective around docks or overhanging trees, it provides much less value on the open water when a *long cast* is needed to get a crankbait down to 25-30 feet of water. When you are asked as a leader to quickly scale up a new team, practicing the art of effective delegation will far better serve you than an internal (and individualized) drive for results. Continually understanding and strengthening the skills related to these casting techniques will serve as the foundation for growth on your leadership journey. Because your legacy starts and ends with you, you first must strive to better yourself before you are fully capable of developing others. You must lead by example before expecting others to follow.

Your goal as a leader is to continue to improve upon each of these casting techniques over time. Remember it will take time—becoming a great leader doesn't happen overnight, nor should it. It's the long game that builds the perspective and skill set that can be utilized across a wide variety of situations. Naturally, there will be certain leadership skills that come easier to you than others. Do not become overly fixated with perfecting any one of these casting techniques, inhibiting you from moving on and growing in another. Remember that leadership is not synonymous with any one skill, but rather the application of many.

Your objective in this chapter is to reflect and identify which casting techniques are your natural strengths and which ones you need to continue developing to help round out your leadership ability. Fair warning, this is the longest chapter in the book, so don't get frustrated if you feel like you aren't moving through the *C.A.T.C.H. & Release* Model fast enough. Feel free to skim and scan as you choose, and please don't allow the inability to fully master one casting technique discourage you from developing others. In fishing, you don't have to know every casting technique to catch fish, but the more versatile you are, the more successful you will be across all situations. The same logic applies to leadership— and music—for that matter. Our friend Jimi didn't need to master playing the drums in order to be a brilliant musician, he just needed enough awareness and understanding of them to create harmony.

Casting Technique #1: Adaptability

The ability to quickly modify behavior to meet changing needs.

Embracing change may be the most difficult, yet greatest lesson to learn in a lifetime. How is it that one ever truly becomes comfortable being uncomfortable? How does one gracefully change course from a path known to a path unknown?

The concept of adaptability has become increasingly important to leadership in recent years, and for good reason. The speed, complexity, and ambiguity that now fill the daily lives of leaders leave them no choice but to adapt or get left in the dust. Leaders at all levels need to anticipate changes in their environments, be willing to adjust when presented with adversity, and learn quickly regardless of the situation. The ideas, tactics, and strategies that worked yesterday are not guaranteed to work today, and who knows what tomorrow will bring. As an effective leader, you will be required to modify your behavior to meet changing needs—there is no way around it.

In fishing, there is a common saying among anglers on how best to select a lure for any given situation. The saying is *"match the hatch,"* and it refers to an angler's ability to replicate the current environment the fish are relating to. To increase the likelihood of a strike, anglers need to observe and process all of the changing environmental cues (weather, water clarity, available prey, time of year, etc.) to put themselves in the best position to succeed. Your ability to successfully lead through challenging leadership situations is no different. You must become an astute student of your environment, the decisions you make, and how you handle change.

So often, our daily routines have a way of blinding us to the subtle changes that are constantly happening around us. The best way to anticipate change is to first understand what is unique about any given moment. Instead of thinking to yourself: *"It's just another Monday morning at the office,"* pick up on the subtleties that make that particular Monday unique. For instance, where you parked, who you greeted when you entered the building, what's on your agenda for the day, and what is different about this Monday from the last. By building greater awareness around you, you will begin to notice small changes that over time turn into big changes. Without this heightened awareness, change may seem to occur more rapidly than it actually unfolds. In fishing, an entire season doesn't change overnight. Slowly throughout the course of several days, small changes occur in the natural environment that transform the entire fishing pattern for a given season. If you take time to observe the changes and make small adjustments to your tackle box and fishing approach along the way, you can still be successful through the changing season. If you don't adapt, you will soon find yourself snagged and feeling like you need to do something drastic to catch up—like buying a new boat or overhauling your equipment and tackle in order to stay relevant amidst the change. While the knee-jerk reaction may give you a sense that you are adapting to the new situation, it is often costly, short-lived, and ineffective in the wake of change.

But what about those times when you feel like you have been proactive and observant of your environment, yet feel like you are not getting the results you want? In fishing (especially from shore), there is another popular saying, *"If you haven't had a bite in 15 minutes, it's time to move."* At one point or another, someone has probably told you that the definition of insanity is doing the same thing over and over again while expecting a different result. The truth of the matter is as the world around you changes, you too must be changing at an equal or faster rate to stay relevant. The way to do this is to open yourself up to trying new approaches, listening to new ideas, and stop being afraid to fail. Fishing a new spot or trying a new technique likely isn't going to make or break your success any given day, but it may provide you clues about the environmental changes and prepare you for future success. Adaptability is all about fighting that inner voice that tells you to stay fishing the same way you always have for another 15 minutes when you have already been there for an hour. If you are willing to constantly move and try new approaches, I promise that you will be better prepared to handle all of the unpredictable challenges leadership throws at you.

As creatures of habit, most of us will fall back to the mode of operation we are most comfortable with. Instead of feeling guilty when you fall back into old patterns, build greater awareness and ask better questions. Challenge yourself by asking, *Am I doing what is comfortable or what is truly needed based on my current environment?* Are you really listening and willing to learn new techniques to *match the hatch* of your audience? How soon is too soon to move on from failure? What can you start learning today that will pay the greatest dividends in the future? As a leader, you not only need to become comfortable with change, you need to proactively seek it. The moment things become too comfortable around you is usually the tell-tale sign that you are ready for your next challenge.

How Have You Successfully Navigated Change In The Past?

Take a moment to think about some of the major milestones in your life with the gift of hindsight. You may have forgotten how much change you actually endured to make your goals become a reality. Whenever I become overwhelmed with change in my life, I intentionally remind myself of all the times that I had successfully navigated change in the past. Back in 2016, my wife and I sold 80% of our belongings, said goodbye to the life we created in Ohio and moved to California. This change seemed pretty scary at first—and it was—like most worthwhile changes in life. It wasn't until I reminded myself that I had already moved to a new state and started over multiple times before that I regained my confidence. Looking back now, the move to California doesn't seem scary at all in comparison to the other upcoming changes in my life. I've grown my adaptability muscle over the years, allowing me to take on bigger changes at an even faster rate in the future. The term psychologists use for this phenomenon is called *self-efficacy* and it refers to our confidence to succeed in the future. Plainly put, self-efficacy grows when we are able to recognize that we have already had similar successes in our past. If you have examples where you have navigated changes well in the past, use that to your advantage before telling yourself all the reasons why a particular change is too difficult.

Like the wind, your environment will continue to change. Embrace these adaptations as a way to strengthen your own self-efficacy. Begin viewing change as an opportunity to catch something new, not threaten something you've caught in the past.

Casting Technique #2: Emotional Intelligence
The ability to accurately interpret, regulate, empathize, and respond to the emotions in oneself and others.

In life, knowing when to speak and when not to speak is a skill that cannot be underrated. Imagine for a moment that you are out on the water fishing with a friend. It has been a long day, the fishing has been slow, and frustration is starting to set in. Although you both are dialed in and focused on catching fish, nothing seems to be working. The optimistic tone of the morning has evaporated, and both of your facial expressions point to signs of defeat. All of a sudden, you notice your friend has just hooked into what appears to be a really nice fish. As your friend reels in, you remain quiet and look to assist in any way you can. You grab the net and just as your friend pulls the fish next to the boat, the fish spits out the lure causing your friend to lose the catch. What do you say at that moment? Do you quickly try to diffuse the situation with your friend and say, *"I guess it's just one of those days!"* Or do you opt to soften the situation by saying, *"Don't worry about it, there are more fish out there."* What if I told you either response could make the situation better or worse depending on the emotional cues from your friend? A situation like the one described above requires a high degree of emotional intelligence to navigate the circumstance successfully.

The term emotional intelligence was popularized by Daniel Goleman in the 1990s and has played an important role in leadership development ever since. Core components of emotional intelligence include having the ability to accurately interpret the emotions of yourself and others, being able to self-regulate your own emotions, and the ability to show empathy for others. All of these components are incredibly important for a leader. Emotions influence our perceptions, decision-making ability, and our ability to build relationships. Understanding how to read others and how our emotions may be coming across helps us determine which behaviors are appropriate and which ones are not for a given situation. The day your friend loses a nice catch on an already frustrating afternoon may not be the best time to immediately point out the obvious by saying something like, *"Ha! That sucks bro!"* A better approach may be to wait a moment and observe your friend's reaction. Once you gather some initial data on your friend's disposition (e.g. tone, body language, etc.), you will be better positioned to adapt your message in a way that better aligns with the situation and the emotions of your counterpart. To do this effectively requires you to regulate (or control) your initial impulses, take a moment to interpret the cues, put yourself in your friend's shoes, and respond in a way that is appropriate for the situation.

Now let's fast forward the script 20 minutes after your friend just lost that fish. Out of nowhere, you feel a giant thump on your line, your rod tip bends down, and the drag begins to peel. As you feel the strength of a fish battling below the surface, you carefully reel in and let line out as needed to secure the landing of this fish. After several minutes of jockeying back and forth, your friend grabs the net and scoops up your prize by the side of the boat. With your adrenaline pumping and excitement coursing through your veins, how do you react in the heat of the moment? Do you let the thrill of the catch get the best of you and roar out a battle cry? Do you instead grab your phone right away thinking about how many likes this fish is going to get on social media before thinking to thank your friend for assisting with the net? Given this situation, can you honestly say with confidence that you would take time to truly soak in the moment, check in to see where your friend was emotionally, and say something meaningful? Even though your emotions are running high, you must be conscious of bragging—it may create animosity and resentment in your friend who just lost their fish. You also can't just go mute—your friend will be expecting some kind of response to the catch. How do you know what is appropriate behavior and what is not? It all comes back to having strong emotional intelligence, being able to survey your surroundings and adapt your emotions/reactions based on the given cues.

As a leader, you will be looked at during times of uncertainty. You will experience strong emotions and have to differentiate rational from irrational thoughts. You will need to show empathy and read the emotions of others in order to build strong relationships. You will need to self-reflect and ask yourself why you feel the way you do in order to establish good emotional health. As much as you may want to avoid emotional situations, telling yourself, *"Emotions don't belong at work"* or *"That's an HR issue"* it likely won't be very helpful to the way you lead. Don't be blind to the truth that emotions are an inevitable part of leadership. Embrace the fact that humans are complex and emotional beings. As challenging as emotions can be to deal with as a leader, they also provide a beautiful zest to life.

The next time you go fishing with someone (or lead someone through an experience), I encourage you to pay closer attention to the emotional cues you send and receive and how they impact the overall experience for you and others. Choosing the right words at the right time and delivering them with a sincere level of empathy can make a world of difference. Don't be the leader who puts others down for your own personal gain by making insensitive remarks. Don't gloat about your accomplishments when others are in no mood to listen. Instead, spend time throughout your day trying to recognize how mild or extreme your own emotions are (e.g. using 1-10 happiness scale). Take a moment to breathe and soak in your environment periodically before you say or do something impulsive. Before making assumptions, consider what others might be experiencing in their own lives that is making them behave the way they are. Try to respond in a way that takes into account the emotions of those around you. Use the information from your environment as a filter to channel your own thoughts and emotions with greater alignment when you speak. Lastly, self-reflect on the situations that evoke a strong emotional response in you, because we all have things that make us tick. Heightening your awareness to these instances will lead to better self-regulation of your emotions down the road.

Casting Technique # 3: Authenticity

Behaving in a way that is genuine with one's own natural tendencies.

You can't fake leadership. Even with the best stage, script, and appearance, people will quickly detect your facade, undermining your effectiveness as a leader. Instead of telling yourself you need to lead like someone else, try leading like *you*. The key is in finding what your unique leadership gifts are—the elements that no one else can replicate. The greatest role you can ever play on the leadership stage is the part that you play yourself. This doesn't mean that you won't need rehearsals, costume changes, stellar performances, and feedback from a director, it just means you will never be as successful trying to lead like someone else over yourself. Continue to seek advice from others, hone your skills, and learn new techniques, but always translate the script back into your own language so your audience knows it's you. You have to keep it real as a leader. It's virtually impossible to build trust and establish lasting relationships without being your authentic self. One of the most liberating moments in your leadership journey is the moment you fully accept yourself. And I mean fully accept everything—the strengths, weaknesses, failures, and imperfections that make you, you. When this shift occurs, it's like the weight of the world is lifted from your shoulders. There is no longer the need to put up a front or behave in any disingenuous ways that others can see plain as day.

Lead Like You

It is so crucial that you don't fall into the trap of trying to be the leader others want you to be, instead of being the leader you were meant to be. For some people, it takes great mental effort to silence judgments from others; however, once you let go of your ego and begin embracing the beauty of who you really are is the exact moment your leadership ability catapults to the next level. Doing this will require you to show some vulnerability. People want to follow leaders they see as human. It provides them a level of comfort knowing that they too can be human in front of their leader. This authenticity will motivate them to go the extra mile without the fear of judgment and build incredible trust among the team.

Many times leaders are made out to be superheroes with extraordinary strengths, and I would argue that leaders are superheroes but likely not for the reason you may think. Take a minute to consider some of your favorite superheroes. Maybe it's Batman, Wonder Woman, or The Incredible Hulk. The one thing all superheroes have in common is that they all possess at least one unique superpower or strength. Equally as important, yet much less emphasized, is the fact that each one of them possesses a human flaw they need to overcome. It's for this exact reason people relate to superheroes even if they possess incredible superhuman powers. Leaders, in a lot of ways, are just like superheroes. We expect them to do unbelievable things, yet we want them to resemble part of ourselves. In doing so, it gives us hope that maybe we can have the same impact they do someday.

The human element, or connection which binds humanity together, is something that no robot will ever be able to replicate because it's in our DNA. Being your humanly self and having the ability to be vulnerable is a beautiful thing. As humans, we all seek some form of approval, security, and control in our environments. Knowing this common thread that connects us all, why is it still so hard to let our guard down and allow others to see our true colors? Perhaps it has something to do with all the craziness we let swirl in our own heads?

For as beautiful as the human mind is, it sure seems to enjoy sorting through a lot of useless minutiae throughout the day. Why do we agonize over hypotheticals, overanalyze the crap out of things, and entirely overestimate the accuracy with which others will notice the same details that consume so much of our conscious thoughts? A few months back a colleague of mine shared with me that she was disappointed when another colleague, whom she worked closely with, didn't notice that she bought and wore five new work outfits one week. Given that these two worked side by side, she thought her new wardrobe would be so obvious that the fellow colleague would mention something, but alas, no compliment was given. This example highlights a psychological phenomenon known as the *spotlight effect*.

The spotlight effect is the mental process by which we overemphasize the degree to which people notice our appearance as though we are being viewed in a spotlight at all times. This term was coined in 2000 after Tom Gilovich and his colleagues discovered that college students continually overestimated the likelihood their peers would notice if they were wearing an embarrassing t-shirt (Barry Manilow) or a non-embarrassing t-shirt (Bob Marley, Jerry Seinfeld, or Martin Luther King Jr.) In both cases, the individuals wearing the t-shirts in college lecture halls overestimated the number of fellow students they thought who would notice their t-shirt (Mendoza-Denton, 2012).

The leadership takeaway from this experiment is to understand that you may not be under as big of a spotlight as you perceive in your own head. It's OK to be yourself and even show vulnerability at times as a leader. Keep in mind that other people will likely be consumed by their own thoughts, goals, and insecurities—so much so that they likely won't even notice that tiny coffee stain on your shirt that you are agonizing about as you present. Try limiting the amount of time you spend in your own head thinking about minor details that will likely go unnoticed. When you allow your ego to govern your thoughts and behaviors, you will miss opportunities to build authentic relationships and enjoy the present moment as your authentic self.

Casting Technique # 4: Continuous Improvement
The mindset that one can continually learn and develop to create a better version of themselves.

As a leader, if you don't believe in continuous improvement or a growth mindset, you should stop reading this book. Pick up whatever activity you were doing prior that wasn't helping you develop into a better version of yourself. If you think your best days are behind you and personal development is a waste of time, you really won't enjoy the rest of this book anyway.

Since you are still reading, I'll take that as confirmation that you believe in lifelong development. Kudos to you for believing that every day offers a new opportunity to get better. Perhaps Rick Clunn, Bassmaster Pro, said it best in 2016 after becoming the oldest angler to win a Bassmaster Elite event at the age of 69. *"Never accept that all of your accomplishments are in the past. Most of us go through a peak period. But when you start to lose that, you start to wonder maybe I don't have as many great moments ahead, but I still have great moments to look forward to"* (Pichhartz, 2016). Three years later (2019), at the age of 72, Rick won his 16th Bassmaster Elite event on St. John's River, FL. True to his words, he celebrated this victory on the same stage he shared his wisdom just a few years prior.

Although the concept of continuous improvement (or self-actualization) is not new, some people continue to choose to have a grim outlook toward their own development. It usually sounds something like this: *"Back when I used to be able to"...* or, *"Maybe in a different life"...* Other varieties sound like this: *"I'm too old for that"...* or, *"I missed my chance a long time ago."* These limited thoughts can prematurely cap potential, doing a huge disservice to the minds they consume. Instead of focusing on development as a lack of current ability, begin to see it merely as an opportunity to get better. Our brain is remarkable, and what it focuses on grows. A leader who focuses on continuous improvement and proactively invites new experiences will indeed end up developing. Call it a self-fulfilling prophecy, the *Law of Attraction*, or whatever else you want to, just know that the mind is powerful and the way you frame your thoughts shapes your life.

Shift Your Paradigm, Shift Your Life

If you struggle with framing your reality, work on flipping the paradigm from *I'm inadequate because of my skill gaps* to *I have opportunities all around me every day to develop my skills.* Remove the pressure to be perfect and focus on incremental progress. The great beauty of leadership development is it's the gift that keeps on giving. There will never be a time that you feel like you have it fully mastered, and that's OK. Ask any professional golfer or angler if they have mastered their sport and see what type of response they give you. In life and in leadership there is no such thing as complete mastery, but there is such a thing as continuous improvement one day at a time.

As a leader, you will gain a lot of respect from your team when you start acknowledging that you are not perfect. Perfection is not the goal of leadership; the goal of leadership is to continuously better oneself and those around them.

Always keep an open-mind toward development. Before limiting yourself with all the reasons why you can't do something, consider all the opportunities you have to gain by trying. There is no expiration date on human learning, that shit's good for life.

Casting Technique # 5: Perseverance

The unwavering strength and determination to achieve goals despite challenges and setbacks.

How long does it take to pull yourself back up with grace when you fail? Because as a leader, you will fail more often than you succeed. Failure is not a matter of if, just a matter of when. I've always said that how a person responds to a loss says much more about their character than how they respond to a win. Of course, both scenarios require a level of sportsmanship, but one cuts deep and the other leaves you tickled pink. Turning pain into passion requires perseverance, and leaders with strong perseverance can fight through setbacks and adversity ferociously.

Here is a hypothetical I want to pose to you that I derived from a TED Talk in 2015 (Hartley, 2015). Given the choice, would you be more inclined to follow a leader who possessed unmatched perseverance or unmatched pedigree? I know it's a difficult question to answer, and part of you wants to say, *"It depends..."* but if you had to make a decision to follow a scrappy leader or an Ivy League leader, who do you think you would pick? If you can't answer that or think it's an unfair question, let me rephrase. Which leader do you believe would be best positioned to lead in the digital age: a leader with an Ivy League degree, 4.0 GPA, wears a designer suit and plays polo on the weekends, or a scrappy leader who graduated from the public university of hard knocks, is hungry to learn, has something to prove, and prefers to take the stairs instead of the elevator? While both leaders now find themselves in the same role, their journeys are very different. The Ivy League leader may have the look, vocabulary, and brainpower to be an effective leader, but may not be battle-tested when dealing with adversity, criticism, or setbacks. The scrappy leader may lack the eye-catching qualifications of the position but may possess the grit to accept feedback, adapt quickly, and continually succeed despite all the odds. The scrappy leader is the type of leader who wins respect through their ability to double down when the going gets tough. Please note that I have nothing against Ivy League graduates. Ivy League graduates work extremely hard to get accepted into and graduate from prestigious schools. Hard work is hard work—through and through. My point is rather that appearance or words on paper can buy some initial credibility, but lasting credibility in the leadership world comes from perseverance.

On your journey, you will inevitably have *one of those days*. The type of day when nothing seems to go according to plan and no matter how hard you try, you continue to come up short-handed. The type of day that frustration accumulates and you get to the point of quoting that notorious line from the movie *Half Baked*, *"F-you, F-you, F-you, you're cool, I'm out"* (Simonds, 1998). In these moments, great leaders choose to persevere, they find a way to turn crap into scrap.

Well, I had one of those days on the water back in 2010. On what felt like the hottest and muggiest day of the entire summer, my parents came to Iowa City, IA to take me out fishing on Lake McBride. Having fished at Lake McBride before, paired with the benefit of fishing from Dad's boat (a treat for any shore angler), I was dialed in to make the most of the occasion. The morning was slow—really slow—like the no-bite kind of slow. We were having trouble both locating where the fish were and also what pattern they were on. The silver lining to the slow morning, and any slow day fishing, really, was the opportunity for us three to spend quality time catching up on our personal lives. A large portion of the conversation was spent talking about my next academic adventure in Minnesota, the transition, the graduate program, and how I was feeling about it.

After a frustrating morning fishing on the north side of the lake, we decided to head to the south side for the afternoon. Now, up to this point, Dad and I were trying all sorts of different lures, and Mom was sticking mostly to her go-to blue ribbon tailed plastic worm we call the "*Marty Worm*," named after my uncle Marty. As for me and Dad, we tried spinnerbaits, crankbaits, shaky heads, swim jigs, buzz baits, and of course, my favorite creature bait called a sweet beaver. It got to the point that it didn't matter what we were throwing, we simply were not having any luck. As our confidence waned and the heat intensified, I decided to go back to my bread and butter—my black and blue Texas-rigged sweet beaver. Having gone through nearly every lure in my tackle box, it was the lure that gave me the most confidence during the angst of confusion. Given how the day was progressing, I knew it was just going to be one of those days where a slower, more methodical approach would be my only bet to land a fish.

Early afternoon, unfortunately, was panning out to be no different than the morning—slow. Mid-afternoon rolled around and Mom and Dad started getting occasional nibbles on their plastic worms that eventually turned into a small bass or two, which was great for them, but just added to my own frustration. Under the hot sun and bluebird skies, my doubt continued to increase. Stiffness in my back and arms started to set in from standing on the boat all day casting what felt like 1,000 casts. All of a sudden, in the midst of my frustration—whack! A strong bite sent my rod tip for a nosedive. Caught slightly off guard, I took a second and went for a strong hookset. Swing... and a miss! The fish was not on the other end. My blood was boiling, it took every ounce of mental energy not to go into a full-on *Happy Gilmore* tirade. In that precise moment, I had a decision to make, and as much as I wanted to throw my pole down and quit, I stayed with the retrieval of the cast, slowly bouncing my lure off the bottom of the lake. I hoped with every fiber of my being that fish would come back and hit my lure again. I was dialed in for my next chance, should it come, and just like that, Smack! The fish crushed my lure and I was ready this time! I set the hook like a pro and kept my rod tip up. The fish fought hard, and I immediately knew it was a giant. Trying my hardest to keep my line tight and avoid any obstructions that may snap the line, I was finally able to land the beauty. She may not have been the biggest fish I had ever caught in my life but was every bit of 20 inches and between 4-4.5 lbs., which is a great fish in a northern state like Iowa.

The roller coaster of emotions and the triumph of landing that fish made my entire day. It was the only fish I caught during an 8-hour outing, but worth every second. My perseverance paid off and, to my surprise, my parents sent the photo of me holding the fish into the local news station for a weekly segment they produce called, *"John's Big Ol' Fish."* Ever since I was a little kid I wanted so badly to make John's Big Ol' Fish, and, on that hot, humid day in 2010, perseverance paid off in the form of a lifelong memory we all enjoyed right before I moved away for grad school.

What makes this story even more symbolic was that same summer I persevered through my own personal adversities. Having graduated from the University of Iowa in the top 5% of my class during the height of the economic recession in 2009, I had to swallow my pride and take a job making $5.15 an hour plus tips as a pizza delivery driver. I couldn't believe that all my hard work, good grades, and countless hours spent being a research assistant led me to the same outcome I could have had when I was 16. I applied to countless jobs, had multiple interviews, yet continued to come up short-handed. I knew I had to make a decision: I could sit there and feel sorry for myself, just like I was tempted to do when I missed that first bite on Lake McBride, or I could take a chance and attend a new university, in a new state, studying a new type of psychology (Industrial-Organizational). During that hardship, I rose above my feelings of shame and channeled my energy toward a new opportunity. One that would lead a pizza delivery guy to follow his dreams by writing this book and launching a business focused on developing others.

The concept of perseverance in leadership cannot be underestimated. Every leader fails, every leader has those frustrating days when nothing seems to go right and they want to throw in the towel. Yet, great leaders always find a way to move forward. They are able to see beyond the setback, embracing that setbacks are part of the journey. They know that the most worthwhile endeavors in life require mental toughness. I will never forget what one of my favorite professors from graduate school told our class one day during a lecture. He said, and I paraphrase, *"I bet there has yet to be a time in your life that you have ever been completely pushed to your mental limit."* At the time, I thought he was just preparing us for our next major project or trying to downplay the workload of that class. Reflecting back today, I can honestly say I have yet to reach my mental limit in what I can achieve, and that mindset all comes back to perseverance. If there's a will, there's a way—you just need to discover what your will is, and your perseverance will find the way.

Casting Technique # 6: Inspirational Influence

The ability to influence others by connecting personal experiences to emotions resulting in an increased commitment to act.

When was the last time you heard a speech that really moved you? The kind that sent chills throughout your body, generating hope and a commitment to action? What was it specifically that impacted you so deeply? How was the speaker—who you may have known very little about—able to conjure up such strong emotions through their words? What was the spark that influenced you to act?

At its core, leadership is largely regarded as your ability to influence others. Understanding this concept is easy for most leaders to grasp, but the execution is what makes the difference in inspiring action. While many influential methods exist, not all are created equal. You have probably encountered some leaders who heavily rely on the *carrot* (positive incentives) or *stick* (punishment) method to influence others. In leadership theory, this method is referred to as *transactional leadership*. The concept is rooted in the idea that a leader can gain compliance (or control) of a follower's behavior through positive or negative transactions. Typically, this type of leader views individuals as robotic commodities in the sense that they have a job to do and based on their output, the proper transaction (carrot or stick) will motivate their performance. There is nothing new about this method, and I'm not saying that it can't be effective in the short-term; however, when it comes to effective, long-term influence, *transformational*, not *transactional*, is more effective. *Transformational leadership* is rooted in the idea that leaders are most effective in influencing positive change when they gain commitment of others through a shared vision, providing ongoing encouragement, and role modeling the same behaviors they seek those on their teams to display. A transformational leader is able to tap into team members' *intrinsic motivation*. Intrinsic motivation refers to the internal drive people have to act without the need for extrinsic motivators like money, status, compliance, etc. Ask yourself this, when you are told to do something (extrinsic) versus wanting to do something on your own (intrinsic), what provides you with more fulfillment and commitment to follow through? What provides you with more satisfaction once it is completed? Inevitably there will be times when you will need to do things that you are extrinsically motivated to do. For instance, take out the trash to avoid getting an earful from your significant other. However, as a leader, you will be better served to first fully understand what intrinsically motivates you, and then inspire others to do the same through your messaging. That bonus you dished out for $1,000 last quarter will never feel as special the second time around to your employees. The good news is there is a type of motivation (intrinsic) that is much richer to its core and longer-lasting than most bonuses will ever be. Unfortunately, many leaders will still choose to rely on extrinsic motivators to inspire action. The reason is that it's easier, but great leaders don't opt for what is easier, they opt for what's better.

What Are The Intrinsic Drivers That Motivate You To Lead?

Inspirational influence can be boiled down to three distinct factors: charisma, instilling a personal connection to your audience, and articulating a brighter vision for the future. Keep in mind that there is a fine line between inspiring others and selling to others. Your goal is not to sell to your audience—few people like being blatantly sold to. Rather, leverage the power of intrinsic motivation by inspiring them to decide for themselves, which will result in increased commitment and follow-through.

Charisma is that perfect blend of energy and personality which makes people think, *I have no idea what they're on, but I want a cup of that*. While some aspects of charisma are linked to personality (which is relatively stable over time), there are still other ways you can improve your tone, cadence, and delivery that will result in more engaging communication. The next time you see someone who is charismatic, take note. What is he or she saying or doing that leads others to want to listen? Does it have something to do with the speed of their delivery? Is it the inflection and word choice? Is it the ability to read the crowd and anticipate what they want to hear next that makes their messaging so contagious? Next time you observe it, capture it. Write down specifically the unique behaviors that are making the biggest difference in the speaker's ability to influence others. While it's nearly impossible to change certain aspects of personality (e.g. extrovert vs. introvert), it's not impossible to practice and improve charismatic behaviors. Practice those effective behaviors in front of the mirror or videotape yourself prior to your next big speech. Notice how you are coming across in your delivery and continue to modify your pauses, tone inflection, and non-verbal gestures to engage your audience in a more charismatic manner.

Intimacy is key when trying to influence others. You must instill a personal connection with your audience in order to inspire them to act. If your message has no tie to them, they have no reason to act. There are a number of ways to instill a personal connection. One of the easiest ways is to share a personal story that draws your audience in, something you have lived through that they could easily see themselves living through (if they haven't already). If you are having trouble coming up with an authentic story that you have lived through that ties to your message, have your audience reflect on a third party. This approach is used a lot during political campaigns when a candidate says, *"Let me tell you about a person I met the other day named Jane the Janitor and the remarkable journey she has had."* The reason politicians use these examples so frequently is that it makes their audience feel like Jane's story could easily be their own.

A third tactic, and perhaps most effective, is to create a personal connection directly with your audience by asking them to reflect personally on the topic at hand. Take them on a hypothetical journey where they are in the driver's seat. Help them visualize a solution to their challenge and how the future environment will look just like Martin Luther King Jr. did in his iconic speech *"I Have a Dream."*

Painting a new and colorful picture will require you to have a strong vision. Without foresight, it's difficult to see where you are going, let alone act. As a leader, you will often need to be the person who paints the vision for others who cannot see. You will need to be creative, challenge the status quo, and instill hope in what can be achieved in the future. This doesn't mean that you should be disingenuous with others because you think the vision you have created is what they will want to hear. It has to be authentic or it will lose merit. Whenever you create a vision, you have to truly see and believe it can come true. A great vision should give you some butterflies—that's how you know it's stretching the current status quo. Don't let the butterflies deter you. Instead, focus on the best way to articulate that vision in a vibrant way that appeals to a broader audience.

When thinking about how to improve your influencing skills consider the role storytelling plays in leading others. Stories allow people to relive experiences and offer the opportunity to foster new learning. For thousands of years, stories have been used to spread knowledge, serve as entertainment, and remember those who have passed on. Our brains are wired to process and remember information in the form of stories, so use this mechanism to your advantage. Consider your own storytelling skills and where you have room to improve. While the importance of storytelling is known to us as children, few adults dedicate the time to revisit the skill later on in life.

The reason I bring this up is that storytelling and inspirational influence go hand in hand, as long as the storyteller is credible. I know a few anglers who have a bit of work to do in this department. Somehow the fish in their stories always seem to get bigger, not only the ones they've caught, but especially the ones that got away. Whatever you do, stay credible and find the right level of detail (not too much, nor too little) or your stories will start to fall on deaf ears, instead of energizing others to act.

The Leader's Hippocratic Oath: Lead With Benevolence

Influencing others comes with great responsibility, which is why this construct may produce some uneasy feelings for you. It can be difficult to believe that leaders will influence others for the right reasons when images of heinous leaders using these same tactics to spread hate, fear, and death come to mind. For this very reason, it's so important for leaders to understand their intentions and use their skills to inspire others in a way that will promote a positive difference in this world. As a leader, you not only have the ability to influence, but you also have an obligation to lead others from a place of benevolence. This obligation is a leader's Hippocratic Oath. Before seeking any type of leadership position, you need to clearly ask yourself *why* you wish to lead. Go back and revisit your leadership statement from the intro, and if you skipped over that part, I encourage you to revisit it now because it's a crucial part of your journey. When your *why* comes from a positive place, you have taken a big step in the right direction in becoming a positive and inspirational leader.

Casting Technique #7: Clear Communication

The ability to communicate in a transparent and concise manner; being able to simplify complex concepts into language easily understood by others.

Simplifying complexity, being transparent, and setting the tone are key elements to any leader's success. In a world filled with countless emails, meeting invites, and personal obligations, it's easy to become overwhelmed and disorganized in our communication. As a result, some leaders struggle to find a balance between communicating too much information and at other times, not enough. Over-communication, where too much detail about non-relevant information is conveyed, makes it very difficult for people to understand key points. While some leaders may feel like this practice provides transparency, in reality, they are likely just adding to the confusion. On the flip side, if leaders make too many assumptions and think others know what they know, they may end up under-communicating, resulting in just as many problems—if not more. Without clear, balanced, and timely communication, leaders will continue to struggle in their ability to lead.

Becoming a more effective communicator requires leaders to answer three basic questions. 1.) Which information is most important?

2.) Who is the appropriate audience? 3.) Which channel should the communication be sent from? Unfortunately, leaders do not always think about these three basic questions when firing out communications. Often times, the reactive nature of their day gets the best of them and they make unnecessary communication errors. Be honest with yourself—have you ever been in a situation when you sent an email, but then realized it required a phone call after not receiving a response? How about the time you set a 30-minute calendar invite without an agenda for a topic that could have been resolved with a text message? Breakdown of communication is usually not the result of a failed attempt, it's usually the result of a deficiency in deliberate thinking. For communication to be really effective, it requires a leader to see beyond their own vantage point and consciously put themselves in the shoes of their receiver. Only then can decisions be made about what content, audience, and channel are most appropriate for the situation. This may sound intuitive, but when faced with a million other pressures in a day, it's often forgotten.

When making decisions regarding content, here are a couple of psychological tips that will help you be more effective in your communication. The first is the *rule of seven, plus or minus two*. This rule refers to people's general ability to encode a limited amount of information into short-term memory. Most people can remember seven bits of information (plus or minus two) at a given time. This is one of the reasons why telephone numbers (excluding area code) are seven digits. Comprehension and retention of information are best served in bite-size pieces. Keep this in mind the next time you write a long email. If you aren't concise in your key points, people will likely not retain what it is you want them to remember. The same can be said on slides, with text messages, and really any other form of communication.

Remember that most people have just as many life pressures as you do, so make your messages concise and easy to understand. If a person is unable to encode information into their short-term memory because it's too lengthy, they will be less likely to encode it into their long-term memory. I cannot emphasize this skill enough—***start getting*** *picky about the key messages you want others to remember.*

The next tip relates to the importance of how you start and end your communications. People have a tendency to more easily recall the first and last pieces of information they see and hear. This phenomenon is often referred to as the *primacy and recency effect.* You likely experienced this effect the last time you went to the grocery store and forgot your list. My guess is that you were able to remember the items you wrote down at the top of the list and the ones at the bottom, but were unclear of some of the items in the middle. Knowing this, think about how you can make the most out of your introductions and closings in messages.

My graduate professor used to say, *"boxes and arrows"* whenever he lectured on effective communication. At the time, my classmates and I thought he was joking. Here we were reading textbooks, academic journals, and feverishly taking lecture notes during class and he was talking about boxes and arrows. Over time I realized that his advice could not have been more spot on. The ability to take the most complex concepts, statistics, and ideas, and boil them down to boxes and arrows that anyone can understand is key to clear communication. You can always follow-up with more detail to those audience members who seek additional information, but whatever you do, don't sacrifice the comprehension of the masses by overcommunicating the finest details to a few. Keep in mind that *"boxes and arrows"* will always be easier for your audience to remember than elongated parallelograms and perpendicular line segments.

Word choice plays an important role in communication. Using words that show off your exquisite vernacular should be saved for your next game of Scrabble. In the leadership world, being understood pays much greater dividends than being sesquipedalian. Using common words that reinforce a strategic vision and shared values unifies teams. When possible, use helpful examples and metaphors to simplify complex problems allowing your audience to draw the connection (e.g. fishing metaphors to reinforce leadership principles). Being the smartest person in the room or having the largest vocabulary won't amount to much if you don't have a team that can execute on a clearly communicated vision.

To Communicate More Effectively... Listen

Last, but certainly not least, do not make assumptions about what your audience does or does not know. Instead, ask questions and listen. Learning how to become a great listener will significantly improve your effectiveness as a communicator. It will allow you to craft and deliver better messages that will connect with your audience in a more meaningful way. Start by picking up on the cues, sentiment, and core topics important to your receiver(s). Remember that communication is a two-way street. If you want people to listen to you, you first must be willing to listen to them. If you desire others to speak up and ask questions, you must also be willing to speak up and ask questions. Lead by example in your own communication style, and others will begin to mirror your behavior.

Casting Technique #8: Courage

Displaying the strength to act during situations of uncertainty, especially when others refuse to act.

Everyone has been there... The time when you should have stepped up, said what you needed to, or did the right thing when no one else would. Regardless of the justification (e.g. someone else should do it, I don't want to be embarrassed, etc.), you convinced yourself it was better to conform than to display courage. Looking back on your inaction, you likely vowed from that point on to never let that same passive behavior happen again. This new promise removes the guilty pit in your stomach initially, but then next time comes all too sudden and you feel that same awkward pressure to conform again and again.

Great leaders have a knack for stepping up when no one else does. They know when and how to flip the script in order to take ownership of a situation—not because it's easier, but because they know they must. Conformity is a powerful mechanism. It shapes human behavior in more ways than people realize. Conformity has the ability to strengthen group efforts, yet it can also be catastrophic when left unchecked. Great leaders are well aware of this social pressure and continuously seek ways to better understand the phenomenon.

Courage And Conformity Go Hand In Hand

Classic social psychology studies like the ones performed by Solomon Asch in the 1950s have shown that under pressure, people would rather conform to a norm than confront a group with a counter-argument. One experiment, in particular, commonly known as the *Line Experiment*, used two different cards with various lengths of lines drawn on each of them. One card possessed three lines on it, a short, medium, and long line. The other card possessed a single line that was a perfect match to one line on the first card. When held side by side, it was quite obvious to the naked eye which line was the match. The experiment consisted of several round-robin exercises where every individual in the room, one by one, would have to indicate which line segments they thought were the correct match. The twist was, prior to a new participant entering the room, a group of confederates (the psychological term for individuals playing a role in an experiment) would agree to unanimously respond with a wrong answer after a few rounds of playing the game. An experimenter would solicit several incorrect answers from confederates and then ask the participant which line they thought was the correct match. You can imagine the tension this created for the participant. Say the right answer, and you may rock the boat with the group. Or comply with the norm and just agree with the wrong answer when you know deep down inside it's wrong. It's quite easy for us to speculate what we would do in that situation, but much harder to go against the grain in reality. Needless to say, Solomon Asch was able to demonstrate the profound impact conformity has on human behavior when internal pressures to fit in intensify. (Asch, 1951).

As a leader, it's important to realize that there are pressures to conform absolutely everywhere—from social platforms, to the clothes you wear, even the toothpaste you choose to use... (after all, 9 out of 10 dentists recommended it, right?) Whenever a group of people are present, the powers of conformity will be at play, so you must be intentional in how you choose to lead.

Pluralistic ignorance, the psychological sibling of conformity, is a phenomenon that refers to our tendency to think that groups of people behaving in similar ways must possess more knowledge or information than ourselves. Said differently, the collective behaviors of a group will result in people making assumptions (often false) that the group knows more about a situation than any single person—following the crowd for crowd's sake instead of thinking for oneself because the crowd *"must know something."*

A professor and I from Minnesota State University published a journal article in 2016 that examined the role social influence had on students' evacuation behaviors during fire alarms in college dormitories. We found that participants in the study indicated a high likelihood of surveying others' behaviors in their own response to alarms, suggesting they looked to others to inform their own actions instead of acting independently (Leytem & Stark, 2016). This effect not only occurs during emergency situations but every day. People model the behaviors of others because it is often easier than walking their own path. Challenge yourself when you start having thoughts like, *Well, everyone else seems to do it that way, there must be a good reason behind it.* In public when you see long lines, don't immediately assume the masses of people know something more than you. Of course, there will be times when the crowd does know something you may not. I am not suggesting to never pay attention to a crowd, but always be willing to challenge your initial assumptions and think about what you would do in a situation if no one else was there. This will help reduce your likelihood of falling victim to pluralistic ignorance and increase the likelihood of showing courage when others will not step up in a crowd.

A number of factors weigh in on the willingness of a leader to display courage. I understand that no one will ever know the exact challenges you face in your life, no one will ever know all of the skills and potential you possess, and no one will be able to call you up and tell you all the times you should display courage. You, and you alone, are the one who needs to figure out all of the intricacies of your own leadership puzzle. You are the one who needs to step up when others will not. You are the one who gets to decide when to follow conventional wisdom and when to choose your own course. Being the best leader you can be will require you to take risks and display courage. I'm not talking about recklessness or stubbornness, I'm talking about finding your inner strength during times the little voice in your head says, *I'm not so sure, no one else is doing that.* The voice is right, no one else is doing that. That's why it takes courage, the same type of courage that will lead you to some of your greatest accomplishments.

When fishing, it's so difficult not to fall victim to pluralistic ignorance and conformity. More times than not, when anglers see another boat on the water, they assume that boat is on a good spot or must know something they do not. In all reality, they are probably thinking the same thing about your boat as they try to figure out the same fishing puzzle you are. How do you know the other boat is having any luck? How do you know they are even fishing for the same type of fish as you? On the water, it's tempting to want to copy the fishing tactics you see other boats attempting, but I promise you it will always be more rewarding to discover your own spots using your own tactics based on your own knowledge. Again, I'm not recommending you completely disregard what the other boats are doing. Take observation, but don't overemphasize their approach or mimic it out of pluralistic ignorance. Instead, execute your own strategy. The most legendary fishing stories don't usually start with, *One day I was out on the water and I saw a bunch of other anglers doing something, so I copied them and landed the biggest fish of my life.* Fish where no one else will fish, lead where no one else will lead, and display the courage needed to be called a great leader.

Casting Technique # 9 – Decision Making

The ability to thoughtfully process information in a timely manner and accept responsibility for the outcomes of one's decisions.

Making thoughtful and timely decisions with limited information in ambiguous circumstances is no easy skill, but one that every leader can benefit by developing. So much of your leadership journey will be determined by the decisions you make. Some decisions you make will be spot on, while others will be dead wrong. Regardless of the outcome of the decisions you make, you will need to own them. Fully own them. Great leaders don't spend time or energy blaming external forces for decisions they make. They learn, they move on, and they continue fine-tuning their decision-making abilities instead.

In addition to owning decisions, leaders must also be mindful of the amount of time they need to make decisions. They can't afford to act as a bottleneck, spending too much time and energy agonizing between minor details of the choices presented to them. You've heard the saying, and it's so true in leadership, *"over-analysis leads to paralysis."* Leaders need to start getting comfortable with making (and owning) their decisions in a more timely manner. The world is speeding up, not slowing down, so to will the decisions leaders need to make.

To be clear, I am not recommending that leaders rush to judgment. There is a balance that needs to be struck between deliberate thought and swiftness. One of the greatest inhibitors to timely decisions is a tendency for leaders to want to gain consensus from every single person involved, every single time. While seeking a level of consensus is important, it can be crippling to wait until 100% agreement is obtained. Being a leader requires you to make difficult decisions, ones in which difficult messages will need to be delivered. If your goal is always to try to make everyone happy, you will end up making no one happy because of the amount of time you waste spinning your wheels. Again, there is a great balance—at times you will be required to make executive decisions, and at other times you will be required to undergo a more democratic process. There is no one approach that works perfectly in every situation. The answer in deciding which decision-making style you choose will depend on the situation, the players involved, the information you have, and the magnitude of the decision.

Understanding your natural decision-making process, the rippling impact it can have, and the meaningful factors that will guide how and when to make decisions is something you will need to continue to practice throughout your leadership journey. As the speed of business and technology continue to increase, so too will the need for you to make timely and thoughtful decisions. Remember that if you are doing your job as a leader (e.g. sparking change, addressing issues, improving the culture, etc.) tough decisions will continue to surface.

A little while back I watched a TED Talk by philosopher Ruth Chang and I no longer view tough decisions the same way. Chang's perspective helped me understand that difficult decisions, more times than not, simply mean there are multiple options that have equally favorable outcomes (Chang, 2014). Think about it. When a decision is really easy (e.g. would you rather relax outside or go to the dentist today for a root canal?), it requires minimal effort to decide. When a decision is more difficult, though (e.g. accepting a new job offer or staying with your current employer), it typically requires more brainpower. Instead of focusing on the fear of making the wrong choice, what if you viewed the decision as two equal opportunities to experience joy? After all, isn't that what's making the decision so difficult in the first place—you can see yourself being successful in both circumstances? If you didn't, it wouldn't be a tough decision. So instead of agonizing over making the right or wrong call, just listen to your intuition and openly accept whatever decision you make. Each decision, for better or worse, will provide you a learning opportunity. There is no such thing as a perfect decision, so stop searching for it.

I must confess, I often try to make perfect decisions at the bait shop. Stuck between two choices, I usually spend entirely too much time trying to weigh out every possible detail between two lures. The inner commentary usually unfolds something like this in my head:

Last time I was on the water, I caught some nice fish finessing a shaky head plastic worm, so I should probably pick up some more finesse worms. Now, what color was I using? I think they were watermelon, right, well, either way, watermelon is a good all-around color and usually produces fish...

Yeah, but you have a lot of watermelon-colored worms already... are you sure you shouldn't try something new like these hot pink bubble gum-colored worms, maybe the fish would be more likely to bite something they don't see all the time?

Are you kidding me, dude, that looks like something out of a cartoon.

Fine, watermelon it is... but wait, watermelon is so boring, what about green pumpkin? Or... black and blue... oh, look there's June bug!

I love June bug, I'm pretty sure the biggest bass I ever caught in my life was on a June bug-color plastic.

Alright, my mind is made up, it's June bug, I have to have that June bug 7-inch plastic worm.

But wait a second, all my plastic worms are 7-inch, I wonder if these come in the 5-inch variety? Nope, it looks like June bug only comes in 7-inch.

Alright, I need to get out of here ... I'm burning daylight I could be out on the water right now.

June bug...I don't know anymore, that big fish I caught was a couple of years ago. Maybe the fish are on a different color now.
Ok, I got it, I will get one pack of watermelon to cover my bases and one pack of June bug to satisfy my urge to try something I haven't in a while.

Wait, do I even need plastics... I think I have enough already, but what I really need is a new spinnerbait after I lost one last time...

Ten minutes later after scanning all the spinnerbaits, I am having trouble determining what weight of spinnerbait I need based on my current tackle box. I'm also having trouble justifying $10.99 for another shad pattern spinnerbait when I probably have four of them somewhat close to the one I am considering at home already. I tell myself,

You know the thing that sucks about spinnerbaits is one bad cast and there goes $10.99.

As I put the spinnerbait back, I find myself making my way back over to the plastic worms. Feeling frustrated and like I am just wasting time, I grab the pack of watermelon plastic worms. In total, this episode had been about 30 minutes and all I leave the store with is a $2.99 pack of plastic worms. As I walk out to the parking lot, I see my phone has 15 text messages and a missed call from my wife wondering when I'm going to be home. I said it would only take a second. I'm at a loss even trying to explain to her why it took so long. I smile in a sheepish manner and say,

"I think I have a problem, Hunny!"

Our decisions, or lack thereof, can impact those around us. The truth of the matter is that the color of the plastic worm didn't really matter. I didn't have a clear plan or even a real problem I was trying to solve. There were multiple options that were probably equally favorable, and I was entirely in my head way too much. The magnitude of the decision was not really important—it didn't require consensus or the processing of a lot of data—yet still left me feeling frustrated. A little bit of preparation could have gone a long way prior to entering the store. I realize this is a light-hearted example and isn't on the same level as some of the difficult decisions leaders make. But the thought process (or lack thereof) shows how the inability to make effective decisions in a timely manner can have a negative impact on our lives and those around us.

Casting Technique #10: Integrity

Behaving in alignment with high moral standards; doing the "right" thing regardless of the circumstance.

Here's a dilemma for you to consider: Imagine you are fishing a competitive tournament, it's late in the day, and your gut is telling you that you are just a few pounds behind the leader. This tournament means a lot to you. Not only is it on your home lake, but it's also a qualifier for a regional tournament that will be televised next month. With time starting to slip away, you become anxious and decide to head back to an area where you spotted a large fish nesting on a bed earlier in the day. In a final attempt to invoke a strike, you start burning a large crankbait in the area with three large treble hooks. All of a sudden, your crankbait stops abruptly, and it feels like you snagged a log. After a brief second, you realize it's not a snag—this is a giant fish. The fish is ferociously peeling your drag as it thrashes below the water. As your heart starts to race, you meticulously keep tension on the line and reel in ever so lightly so you don't lose this fish. Thoughts of winning the tournament and qualifying for next month's event start flooding your mind. After several minutes of back and forth, the fish finally surfaces. It's a beautiful fish, but to your disbelief, you foul hooked it, snagging it in the tail. The rules of the tournament clearly state that no fish sitting on a bed can be weighed in if foul hooked. A sick feeling hits your stomach as you now come to realize the real reason the fish was fighting so fiercely. It's the biggest fish you have caught all day and you have little doubt it would be the one to put you in the lead. Since no one was with you and there is no blood or evidence of a foul hook, you have a moral decision to make. Do you release the fish, or do you throw it in the livewell and go collect the top prize at your home lake? You don't have much time to decide, the weigh-in starts in 15 minutes and you still need to make it back to the boat launch two miles away.

Solutions to dilemmas like the one I just described seem pretty obvious when they belong to others, but how do they feel when they belong to you? Everyone has been there, whether it's coming across another person's wallet with a wad of cash in it, telling a cashier they gave you too much money back, or filing your taxes in an honest manner. There will always be a small, or maybe even a large part of you, that wants to side with the action that best serves your personal interests. Likely there is also a voice inside your head reminding you what's right and what's wrong. In the end, what do you ultimately decide to do and why?

Integrity. Integrity is the glue that holds all of the qualities of a great leader together. It's the internal compass and good intention to do what is right regardless of temptation. Integrity is what brings nobility to leadership. Without integrity, words become meaningless, trust is thrown out the window, and even the best strategies will be questioned by others trying to figure out your true motive.

As humans, there are times we make the right call, and there are times we make the wrong call. The goal is not to be perfect—you will never be the perfect leader. Instead, focus on strengthening your integrity muscle over the course of your lifetime. Build upon your successes to fight off temptation. Doing so will allow you to hold your head high regardless of the circumstances.

As a leader, you will undoubtedly face a number of moral dilemmas, many of which will be very personal to you and your past experiences. Aspects not only from the past, but the present, and future will also shape the moral lines you draw for yourself. Morality will vary from culture to culture, family to family, and person to person. The question is always the same though: *What is the right thing to do?* Deep down inside you are the only person who can answer that. Following through on what is right, no matter how painful it feels in the short-term, will bring you greater long-term joy and effectiveness as a leader.

Returning back to the foul-hooked fishing dilemma. It's pretty easy for us to tell the angler in the story what to do in that situation. *Release the fish, stupid ... that's a rule violation.* With that being said, it's important for us to realize that from their shoes it's a much harder decision. A real-life example of this dilemma is the heartbreaking story of *Dottie.* Ask any bass angler about Dottie, and they can likely tell you how close Mac Weakley was to becoming the largemouth bass world record holder. Weighing in at 25 lbs.,1 oz, she would have shattered the previous record held since 1932 of 22 lbs., 4 oz! But this isn't a fairytale, and that's not where the story ends. Instead of celebrating, Weakley had to make the ultimate decision: release Dottie back into the water, or try to register her for the record. There was just one small (or rather large) problem. That day in 2006, Dottie was spotted on a nesting bed pre-spawn and foul hooked by Weakley. This means that she didn't actively choose to bite the artificial lure Weakley was using; therefore, Weakley would be ineligible to be entered into the record books. The agony of Weakley's story was exacerbated by the fact that he and his friends had already caught and released Dottie three years prior at a lesser weight. Would anyone have ever known if Weakley decided to lie that day and tried to register her in the record books? We will never know because he decided to demonstrate integrity. He chose to do the right thing and released her back into Dixon Lake, CA. For the next several months one of Weakley's fishing friends was on a mission to catch Dottie, only to find her washed ashore in May of 2007 dying of natural causes. Her body was intact, including that unforgettable dot accenting the bottom of her tail (Carter, 2008).

Leaders have a great platform to model integrity. They should not only display it at the highest degree, but they should also be willing to show compassion when others occasionally do not. While the degree of compassion may be influenced by the severity of the situation and how frequently a particular individual shows the inability to act with integrity, the point is that leaders must remember to recognize their own lapses in judgment before they become overly critical of others. Leaders should help others better understand their decisions, not serve as the moral judge sitting in an ivory tower. In the prior example, they need to help the angler consider what is going to bring greater joy in the long run—winning the tournament today, or living the rest of their life knowing it required the bending of the rules to win. Every time someone congratulates that angler on the victory, comments on the picture where the angler is holding the trophy or asks the angler for advice on how to catch the big one, that decision of integrity will be revisited in the mind of the angler.

Be the leader who doesn't only do what's right when others are watching but also does what's right when others aren't watching. In addition, continue to help others resist temptation and poor decision-making by reinforcing the joy that comes from building a legacy one can be proud of. Explain to others that integrity is like an internal compass; if actions come from a good place, (e.g. wanting to do the right thing for the organization, an individual, or a client), they will find themselves pointed in a direction they can be proud of. As a leader, show them why integrity is important, not only through your words but also through your ongoing actions.

Casting Technique #11: Drive for Results
The proactive pursuit to accomplish tasks and achieve results.

Needless to say, a leader must be willing to get shit done. They must possess an internal drive that serves as the engine powering them through some of their most meaningful career accomplishments. Leveraging an industrious mindset, executing *S.M.A.R.T.* goals (a method covered in a later chapter), and tapping into intrinsic motivation are all required to sustainably achieve results. You already know that leadership is not for the faint of heart. It requires the ability to—day in and day out—wake up with a drive to reach higher and find new ways to achieve meaningful goals. When done right, each day should stretch you, create some discomfort, and leave you feeling like you've emptied the tank. While a drive for results is somewhat a given when discussing leadership, it isn't just about a constant grind, it's also about learning how to drive with focus and longevity.

With good reason, there is a rationale for why you hear about the importance of goals in nearly every professional development workshop you attend or book you read. As I mentioned, we will get into the specifics of *S.M.A.R.T.* goals in a later chapter, but for now, let's focus purely on the power of writing goals down frequently and executing them with consistency. Given the nature of leadership and the speed of the world we live in, it's important to adopt the right mindset when it comes to setting goals for ourselves. If you are like most people, you understand the importance of goals but rush the process, fail to follow through on them, or worse, don't even write them down. It's awfully hard to achieve what you can't clearly articulate. Like most professionals, I used to wait to set my goals once a year around performance reviews. I was letting a corporate process dictate my goal-setting actions. This was not only insufficient, but it also made me resent the entire exercise. Typically, the type of goals created during the review process force leaders into creating goals that *fit* a certain corporate expectation, but often don't align with personal aspirations. While performance goals tied to organizational goals and competency models have their place in organizations, your leadership development will be driven by you—this means *you*—and nobody else.

Do you write in a journal? For the longest time, I used to fight the idea of writing my thoughts and goals down on paper. It seemed so childish and laborious, especially living in a digital world where I could document anything I wanted to on my phone. The problem is I failed to record anything, instead, I was just getting distracted by the million things that can distract you on your phone. After watching my wife write in hers for years, and hearing the benefits others claimed it had, I swallowed my pride and started doing the meaningful work. It doesn't have to be hard, and anyone can do it. Start simple, and soon you will create a routine. For example, set a goal this Monday morning for the week. Try not to view this as another *to-do*, but rather the build-ing blocks to new development that will make you a better leader. This goal can be about anything (relationships, finances, work quality, etc.) as long as it's stretching you to become better. You can have some goals that are short-term and others that are long-term. Ideally, some of your shorter-term goals will align with your long-term goals, thus building your self-efficacy along the way. When you revisit your goals, as you should frequently, don't beat yourself up if you came up short. It's OK. Instead of feeling guilty, reflect on what did and did not help you achieve your goal, and then move on to make new ones. Some words of wisdom: if you achieve every goal you set, you aren't setting your goals high enough. Failure is part of growth and has a way of brewing up some of the strongest internal drive for results there is.

On the flip side, one of the greatest pitfalls I see in ambitious leaders is not knowing how to *turn the engine off*. Most of your life you have probably heard the saying, *"hard work pays"* but in reality, *smart work pays*. Your energy, and what you devote it toward, is very important, not only to the quality of your work but also to your overall health. Burning the midnight oil to maintain a perception of being busy is not displaying a drive for results. The right drive for results is strategic. You will, of course, be required to go the extra mile from time to time, but make sure the extra mile is tied to a meaningful and aligned result. This can be challenging, especially in organizational cultures where a lot of value is put into the perception of being busy as opposed to the accomplishment of meaningful goals. To avoid falling into this trap, make sure you have strategic goals and metrics that can help you decide if the juice is worth the squeeze for any given task. If longevity and sustainability are crucial to your leadership legacy, don't allow your internal drive to result in burnout. Keep the drive alive by being proactive in your ability to set and execute aligned goals.

Ultimately, your objective is to find what naturally kicks your engine into high gear, allowing your passion to drive your results. Through this journey of discovery and execution remember that you are not an all-knowing deity nor a machine, so have compassion for yourself as you hit speed bumps along the way. Going faster isn't always the answer, sometimes you need to slow down in order to keep your vehicle upright. At the end of the day, you know how much gas is left in the tank and when you are driving on *E.* You know the difference between a good day's work when you come home with a sense of accomplishment *vs.* a sense of guilt thinking you had more left to give. Try to approach every opportunity as a chance to better yourself and follow-through on the goals you committed to. Be sure to listen to your body along the way. It does a lot for you, be in tune with what it really needs to run optimally. Always strive for a balance that allows you to achieve your current goals while still having enough energy to enjoy your personal life and relationships. Your internal engine (i.e. drive for results) will lead you wherever you want to go, but if you are unsure of your destination and fail to perform regular maintenance, you may get lost and overheat in the process.

Casting Technique #12: Effective Delegation

The ability to assign appropriate tasks to individuals in a way that promotes development and accountability through the trust that others will carry out tasks effectively.

If you want to be a great leader, stop trying to do it all yourself. At some point or another, your potential will be capped if you aren't able to effectively delegate tasks appropriately. Learning how to effectively delegate allows a leader to focus on what matters most while simultaneously providing others opportunities to develop themselves. Knowing this, why is effective delegation still such a difficult skill for many leaders to learn? For starters, those new to leadership are rarely given the opportunity to practice delegation prior to taking on a new leadership role. In many organizations, lower-level leaders are promoted to leadership positions based on individual performance, not the performance of a collective team. Combine that skill gap with a lack of leadership training provided to less experienced managers (most budgets are spent primarily at the top), and you find yourself in the perfect storm of micromanagement and burnout risk.

Let's face it—as creatures of habit, most people are more comfortable completing tasks they are familiar with rather than entrusting others to complete the same tasks. Couple that tendency with a strong inclination for perfection, and all of a sudden, leaders can't help but find themselves overwhelmed, spending countless hours nitpicking personal preferences vs. providing value add contributions. I can attest to witnessing this regularly early on in my consulting career. People who were several pay grades above me would spend way too much time giving me feedback on the most minor details of my deliverables. Instead of reviewing the content and giving me helpful tools and ideas on how to make the end product more robust, they would ask for control of my laptop and start correcting font sizes and colors. Of course, details are important, but becoming consumed with the most granular of things just to satisfy personal preferences is not a good use of time and can disengage coworkers. This one time, I was facilitating a workshop with a CIO and her direct reports when a senior leader on my team came up to me (while I was facilitating) and pointed out the smallest of typos on the 5th page of the participant packet we were working off of. If I recall correctly, I believe a word was in the present tense when it should have been in the past tense. Regardless, the timing of the feedback and the overall value-add—given I couldn't do anything about it in that moment—was somewhat pointless to deliver right then and there. In the grand scheme of things, the CIO said the workshop was really well organized and she felt her team got exactly what they needed out of it. I know leaders aren't perfect, but when it comes to delegation and feedback (which will be discussed later), it is crucial leaders differentiate and prioritize the most meaningful elements.

Unfortunately, there are still a number of leaders who view their team members as subordinate, lazy, and inadequately trained to do their job. Instead of trying to learn the unique skills and goals of each of their team members, they tend to pick a couple of high performers and dump all the work on them. These leaders have no desire, and in some cases, lack the skills, to properly delegate work to the broader team. In the long run, this hurts everyone and makes it difficult for an organization to scale.

As a leader, you need to empower your team members. Stretch them to take on new challenges and encourage them to learn from their mistakes. Create an environment that promotes trust, acceptance, and growth. The majority of people want to grow personally and professionally at work. They want to get more out of work than just a paycheck. Help them understand how the tasks they are assigned connect to their personal goals as well as the strategic goals of the organization. If you're the type of leader who thinks most people get out of bed wanting to do a bad job, stay stagnant in their careers, and waste company resources, maybe you are the one who needs to change... not them.

The goal for you and the people on your team should be to strive for a state of *flow*. Flow is a concept developed by Mihaly Csikszentmihalyi which defines the experience of being *'in the zone.'* (Csikszentmihalyi, 1997). Have you ever lost track of time because you were so immersed in an activity? The state of flow is experienced at the intersection of a challenge and the ability to perform it. If a task is too easy, people become bored quickly, and if a task is too difficult, people are likely to quit prematurely. When experiencing the state of flow, people are so focused on the task at hand that they don't think about time or even being in the state of flow. The more people experience flow, the more satisfied and fulfilled they tend to be. The goal of a leader should be to provide as many people on your team with the opportunity to experience flow by discovering their *'sweet spot,'* matching their skill sets to the current tasks you can delegate. This takes time, an accurate understanding of the individuals on your team, and the proactive pursuit of finding engaging and purpose-driven work to spread amongst your team. When your team members experience flow, their workday will appear to go by faster, they will be performing at a more optimal level while also developing new skills to better themselves.

———————

As you can see, applying the fundamentals of leadership collectively is a great deal of work. *The 12 Casting Techniques* highlighted in this chapter cover a lot of really good leadership ground that all leaders should revisit from time-to-time. Remember, your legacy as a leader will require you to practice what you preach. Before leaders walk, they crawl, and before they catch, they *Cast Their Line.*

Chapter 2

Attract Diverse Anglers

Diversify Your Network and Challenge Your Understanding of the World

"Every man I meet is in some way my superior, and in that I can learn from him."

-Ralph Waldo Emerson

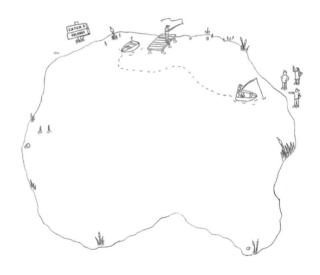

Leadership Constructs Discussed in *Attract Diverse Anglers*
Approachability • Suspending Judgment • Inclusiveness
Curiosity • Diversity of Thought

Fishing on Lake St. Clair that day, I was beyond skeptical. I was convinced there was no way in hell we were going to be successful dead sticking for smallies. I had never fished that way, let alone heard anyone else fish that way in fishing magazines or online. My mind was already made up, but amidst my swirling doubt, I was continuously told we had no other choices due to the windy conditions. My fellow teammate Bob tried to lift my spirits after a slow morning, talking about Hawkeye football and asking me how my older brother who used to also be on the team was doing. It was a nice attempt to cheer me up, but I still was not convinced of our approach. Regardless of my opinion, I stuck to the plan, but in the back of my mind, I thought: *These Michigan anglers have no clue how to fish for smallmouth bass the way we Iowans do.* Then, out of nowhere, *click click click click click*, Bob's drag takes off as he says with excitement, *"Fish On, Grab the Net!"*

After gaining new insights from *The 12 Casting Techniques*, it's now time to strengthen your leadership ability and overall impact by *Attracting Diverse Anglers*. As a leader, you are given both the privilege and responsibility of captaining a boat. Leaving the dock from your new vessel, it doesn't take long to see the advantages your new leadership position grants you. In addition to possessing greater mobility, you also have room to bring others along for the ride. How you choose your company—or better yet—how you attract your fellow passengers, will not only impact your own legacy but will also serve as the mold for others wishing to establish their own. Being a captain requires you to fully understand how your thoughts and actions influence the anglers fishing alongside you. Out on the water, with limited space and battling the elements, it will better serve you to attract passengers who actually want to fish, who intrigue you, and who provide you with just as many learning opportunities as you provide them. The bonds you create on your boat will drive the longevity of your legacy, provide you with lasting memories, and give you great purpose. From the pool of all possible anglers to bring along, keep in mind that there will be some you naturally want to fish with, and others you are not so sure about. Getting those decisions right will be crucial to your success. More days than not, you may be tempted to fish with those who use the same casting techniques as you, but keep in mind that your legacy will ultimately depend on your ability to build relationships with anglers who cast differently than you.

Authentic Relationships:
Genuine Bonds Established Through Mutual Respect And Vulnerability

Build authentic relationships. At one point or another, you have likely heard this advice. If you've never heard it, I'm telling you now—the key to success in nearly every phase of life comes down to your ability to build meaningful relationships in an authentic manner. Relationships play such a pivotal role in our ability to execute business strategies, learn new concepts, and find fulfillment in what we love to do. Relationships allow us to see the world beyond ourselves. They aid in our ability to accomplish more and develop faster through collective efforts. Knowing *how* to develop your relationships and *who* to develop relationships with is quintessential to leadership and the essence of this chapter.

When building new relationships, we typically ask ourselves a very basic question: do we *like* an individual? Unfortunately, this decision is largely determined by superficial factors: appearance, how a person sounds, or even who they remind us of. Naturally, we tend to favor those who resemble our own appearance and likeness, a psychological principle known as the *similar-to-me effect.* There are several reasons why this phenomenon occurs in the minds of humans. First and foremost, it's comforting to know others are like us, it reinforces our beliefs, values, and appearance. From a cognitive perspective, it's easier to fill in the blanks of a new acquaintance who reminds us of ourselves. This bias grants us false permission to make assumptions about a person based on our own beliefs. Said differently, if they sound like me, they probably enjoy fishing and even vote the same party line as me. From an evolutionary perspective, the similar-to-me effect may have aided humans who needed to quickly distinguish members of their own tribe from those of enemy tribes; however, in today's world, leaders who only surround themselves with like-minded people get left in the dust. Building eclectic teams, understanding multiple perspectives, and acquiring new knowledge are all crucial elements to long-term leadership success. That's why the better question to ask yourself is not how much you like a new acquaintance, but what opportunity do you have to learn from them?

At the end of the day, every person has a story to tell. If you are truly willing to listen, a complete stranger has the power to teach you something profound. Similarly, you also have the power to pay forward the great life lessons you've learned with those you meet. Doing this requires you to immerse yourself into parts unknown, just as the late Anthony Bourdain showed us on countless occasions through his adventures in foreign lands. Amongst new acquaintances (especially from different cultures) great gifts reside. My advice to you is to be the *lure* that *Attracts Diverse Anglers* to lead by your side.

THE LURES OF LEADERSHIP

As an angler, the type of lure you cast greatly influences the species of fish you catch. Similarly, as a leader, the mindset and behaviors you demonstrate greatly influence the type of people you attract. Strive to be more intentional with your thoughts and relationships prior to captaining your boat. Thoughts and biases, just like lures, can be dangerous if not handled with proper care, thus, always make a conscious effort to challenge your own mental tendencies. Discussed on the following pages are five lures every leader should keep in their tackle box as they voyage out with new anglers.

Lure #1: Approachability

Behaving in a way that welcomes interactions with others.

Walking into my first University of Iowa Bass Fishing Team meeting is a memory I will never forget. The meeting was held in the basement of Schaeffer Hall in an area known as the Pentacrest on campus. My brother, who was attending grad school at Iowa, informed me that a university club made up of college-age anglers would be hosting their season-opening event there. He said that he had discovered the club online and explained to me that a group of students would get together regularly to discuss, organize, and fish in bass tournaments in the surrounding areas. Later, we found out that the university supported the effort by providing the meeting space and a small stipend to help fund the club which was supplemented by other fundraising efforts like selling t-shirts, hoodies, and jerseys to pay for gas and entry fees into tournaments. Before going into any of the great memories made at the tournaments, it's important for me to share my first experience walking into that initial meeting.

By now you can gather that I grew up enjoying fishing pretty much my whole life. It's been a fun hobby of mine for a long time, but *hobby* is the keyword. I wasn't even close to being on the same level as some of the other members who were seeking to become professional anglers later in life. To be honest, I didn't really understand the bass fishing industry, let alone possess all the high-end gear avid anglers wear. Needless to say, I felt a little like a fish out of water heading into that first meeting.

For those of you who don't really know much about the industry either, the sport is predominantly dominated by the southern states which have the climate to support the sport on a more year-round basis. Even the Bassmaster Elite Series, the highest level of professional bass fishing, is heavily dominated by southern anglers. There are just a handful of well-known professionals from the northern states.

I have to admit that, at first, I fell into the trap of labeling the professional side of the sport as *redneck* and something that probably wouldn't align with my worldview at the time. I had already painted a picture of the type of people who would be at this event and started to get cold feet. When push came to shove, I did actually muster up enough courage to attend my first meeting. Not knowing what to expect and not feeling incredibly confident, I grabbed a chair in the back of the room. Sound familiar? There were roughly 30 students in attendance, including, to my surprise, some female anglers. Remember, I had already made up my mind how this was going to go, the type of people who would be showing up, and the kind of activities I was going to have to volunteer to help with.

Prior to the start of the meeting, the president of the club, Bob (the same guy I fished with on Lake St. Clair), and his vice president Tyler, stood at the front of the room greeting people as they came in. They made sure that all in attendance signed the attendance sheet as they welcomed both new and familiar faces. Now, I have to say, from the outside, many people I grew up with probably thought that this type of club was made specifically for a guy like me. But, to be truthful, at the time I had only fished occasionally in recent years. A number of other hobbies—playing in a band, weight lifting, and socializing—were beginning to take precedence ahead of fishing. Having just wiped the dust off my old fishing gear, I was a little nervous to be surrounded by other anglers repping fishing sponsors on their clothing.

At the top of the hour, Bob and Tyler kicked off the meeting and, to my surprise, the vibe was incredibly warm and welcoming. As they presented the highlights from last year and the schedule of activities for the upcoming year, I became very intrigued. Shortly after, they revealed that they had a surprise for every person who showed up and joined the club that night, a free Fenwick fishing rod and pair of polarized Oakley sunglasses (combined over a $250 value) just for attending. A little fun fact that most people don't know is that a lot of fishing companies like to pilot new equipment with universities to collect feedback. These companies are willing to provide free gear in exchange for feedback from younger anglers related to their products. It's a pretty good deal for college students strapped for cash.

Expectations vs. Reality

Halfway through the meeting, it hit me—my expectations were dead wrong. I had pretty much told myself that I was going to be walking into an episode of *Duck Dynasty*, where a group of know-it-all bass fisherman would be sizing up all of the wannabe city slickers who thought they could fish. In reality, my perception couldn't have been further from the truth. Instead of creating division, the club leaders had a beautiful way of unifying everyone, regardless of background or past fishing experience. There was a common bond that everyone in attendance had—a love for the sport.

Reflecting back, I credit the positive atmosphere and experience of that first meeting to the level of approachability demonstrated by Bob and Tyler. The way they carried themselves and encouraged participation from seasoned and novice anglers alike made me feel comfortable being myself. Keep in mind that both of them were, hands down, the most knowledgeable and skilled anglers in the room—by a long shot. Bob even owned his own bass fishing boat in college! He and Tyler had used that boat to fish around the country the prior year, where they placed in a number of reputable tournaments. They had every right to be pretentious, yet did not show an ounce of arrogance. The two of them were just as eager to learn about the fishing experiences and techniques from others in the club as they were to share their own experiences. They took the time to answer questions and did not belittle someone for not knowing a specific fishing term. They understood that their platform was not about creating a personal fan club for their accomplishments, but rather a forum to help people interested in developing their skills and finding a greater connection to the sport they loved. To this day, I still stay in touch with Bob and Tyler, and even though they may not know how nervous I was that day, they created a lasting memory in me of what it meant to be an approachable leader.

Having observed varying levels of approachability from leaders, I have come to realize that the more approachable leaders are, the more opportunities they have to develop and learn from others. It's really that simple. The more open you are, the more you are able to give and receive knowledge from others. Leaders who remain open to others attract people from all backgrounds. They find innovative ways to tear down walls and bring diverse groups of people together. They make themselves available both physically and mentally. They don't spend the majority of their time behind closed doors nor do they maintain an intimidating persona. They don't act like being too busy for others is a badge of honor. They aren't afraid to make real eye contact with people during situations where it would be easier to look away. These leaders make others feel like they are important in their presence, not invisible. All of these factors play a huge role in trying to build authentic relationships. When you are approachable, others feel comfortable asking the questions they may not have otherwise asked. Being approachable allows for greater understanding and candor between both parties. It allows people of all walks of life to reach out and feel like they will be treated with dignity. Increased approachability promotes the chances someone who is not *just like you* will share an interesting perspective you may never have overwise heard.

Strive to be the leader who sits next to a stranger who would have no idea if you were the CEO or an entry-level employee at your company but is blown away by how approachable you were. When that stranger finds out who you really are, think of how much more willing they will be to listen to what you have to say. Your effectiveness as a leader comes back to the relationships you develop; being approachable is how you start the conversation.

Lure #2: Suspending Judgment

The ability to suspend initial judgment.

Our brain loves simplicity, to the point that it actually craves it. This affinity with simplicity is the result of having to constantly process substantial amounts of information simultaneously. Take, for example, the number of conscious thoughts the average person has in a day. While the exact number may differ from individual to individual, research out of Stanford University suggests the number could be close to 60,000 conscious thoughts a day. Even more striking is that up to 90% of those thoughts may be repetitive (Comaford, 2013). That's roughly 54,000 repetitive thoughts a day, some of which serve you and some of which simply do not. Imagine what reducing the overall number of thoughts could do for your well-being and peace of mind. More so, imagine how your mental health would improve if the repetitive thoughts you had were more positive than negative in nature? We will dive deeper into the power of thought later on, but for now, the main point is that we demand a lot from our brain—both consciously and unconsciously. Regardless of the lifestyle decisions (e.g. sleep, diet, and other choices) we make, we often expect our brain to function as a high-speed processor. Many people fail to provide the brain with the restoration it needs in order to continually perform at an optimal level. Amidst the fog, our brain still has to try to make sense of the madness that is pouring into it at all times. The result: it has to take shortcuts in order to produce quick outputs. While there are methods to reduce some of the noise, which we will discuss later, there is no way around the fact that your brain will continue to use shortcuts. There is, however, a great benefit in understanding some of the shortcuts your brain takes, and how to prevent them from being detrimental to your leadership practice.

Never Underestimate The Importance Of Contextual And Environmental Factors

Imagine you are walking in a heavily urban area, the likes of downtown Chicago or New York City. Immersed in the concrete jungle, you notice a homeless man on the street asking for change. What are your initial thoughts? Be honest with yourself, what are the first shortcuts your brain makes? If you are like most people, you may think that the man has made terrible life choices, maybe he's an addict, maybe he's mentally ill, or maybe he is just lazy. You may even think to yourself: *Instead of looking at me for a handout maybe he should get a job like the rest of us!* Everyone has made judgments like the ones described above, it's human nature. You will never be able to block out thoughts like these completely, but you can increase your awareness of the times when you think this way. To do so requires a better understanding of the psychological drivers behind this mental shortcut.

A question for you to consider is this: what do all of these initial assumptions have in common? They all fail to take into account the contextual or environmental factors the homeless man has endured leading him to that place in time. Our brain can easily recognize the signs of poor hygiene, bloodshot eyes, and a perceived lack of ambition—no problem—but it can't possibly see the whole story. The reason why is simple: it's the result of our brains quickly being able to process surface information, such as the ripped jacket he is wearing or the poor handwriting on the sign he is holding. Being able to gather and process information quickly, while useful at times, leads us to make judgments about the characteristics individuals possess disproportionate to the characteristics of the environment they have experienced. Think about it, what are the pieces of information not readily available for our brain to process? Perhaps one is the fact that the same homeless man is an Afghanistan veteran who has been rejected from two job positions already this week? Another is that he lost his spouse and young child in a car accident several years back which has weighed heavy on his heart ever since. The nail in the coffin is that he hasn't been able to receive the proper medical attention he needs for a disability he received during the war because of a current backlog at the V.A. When presented with all of the information does it still feel fair to place such harsh judgments on a man you may have passed by in a matter of seconds? The ability to suspend initial judgments or, at a minimum, recognize the shortcuts we make when labeling others is a critical component of being a fair and objective leader. Developing this ability takes a tremendous amount of self-awareness, and a desire to challenge our own initial assumptions.

On the water, when a fish jumps from the surface, what's your first thought? Personally, more times than not, I assume that fish is on the hunt for prey. I quickly follow the splash with a cast in that direction. You would likely do the same, too, right? Considering the example above, since we aren't able to see below the surface, it's hard for us to truly know what caused the fish to jump. Perhaps there was a predator is in the area, causing the fish to be spooked. Maybe the fish saw a bright flash from the reflection of the boat? Maybe a motor in the distance just fired up? Regardless of what the real reason is that caused the fish to jump, our initial reaction is based on what we saw, a fish on the surface of the water, which causes us to make an inference about the fish's disposition (hungry, aggressive, etc.). Leaders, unfortunately, do not have the ability to see all of the actions of those they lead, but they do have the ability to think more holistically and suspend initial judgments.

The psychological phenomenon I have been describing is referred to as the *fundamental attribution error*. It's the tendency to attribute behaviors in others to personal factors more than environmental factors. Said differently, we are quick to judge others based on individual characteristics more so than the external factors that may be influencing their behavior. The great irony about this phenomenon is that when it comes to ourselves, we tend to attribute environmental factors for our own behavior more so than personal factors, imagine that. Consider this example. If you see a stranger in public trip on an uneven sidewalk, you likely will think to yourself that perhaps the person is clumsy or uncoordinated. Now, if you had tripped on the same sidewalk, you are much less likely to think, *I'm clumsy*, and more likely to think, *This sidewalk is uneven, everyone can see that*. Once again, it comes back to what you see and what you do not see. In the case of our own trip, we are physically looking at the ground and attribute the outcome to the sidewalk, but not ourselves. When it comes to another person tripping, we see them trip and have the tendency to attribute the behavior to something internal within them. As a leader, you will greatly benefit from your ability to recognize when you are making personal judgments about others without fully accounting for the entire circumstance.

Always Make A Good First Impression

Knowing this now, think of how important first impressions are for this exact reason. Since the majority of people are going to label our behavior to personal attributes more often than environmental factors, try to always place yourself in the best light during a first impression. I know it's not fair to label individuals on initial interactions, but, unfortunately, that's the shortcut many people's brains take. As a consultant, it was far too common that I would hear C-suite executives making label judgments about people moments after meeting them. Teammates would tell me, *"No pressure, but this executive will determine if you are smart or not within the first few minutes, and based on that label, he or she will treat you accordingly for the rest of the project."* From a social perspective, it's unfortunate that we fall victim to this shortcut, but building our own awareness allows us to navigate leadership situations with much more grace. Don't be the type of leader who thinks you've seen it all, allowing you to make personal judgments quickly. Regardless of your experience, every person is unique and deserves a fair shake. One way you can effectively combat the fundamental attribution error is to suspend your initial judgments when meeting others. Refrain from using labels. Don't paint people with broad brush strokes based on political, religious, or cultural views. Allow yourself time to process the entire context and environment a person comes from before dishing out sticky labels that are hard to remove once put out into the open. Think not just about the action above the water, but all of the activity going on below the surface with individuals you lead.

Lure #3: Inclusiveness
Providing equal opportunities for all to participate.

Leaders are faced with inclusive decisions daily. Everything from sending emails, calendar invites, and even where they decide to take their lunch breaks includes elements of inclusion. Building on the concept of the fundamental attribution error, it's easy to see how attributions (both positive or negative) can influence relationships and ultimately decisions of inclusion. When it comes to making judgments about people, the brain will do what it does best and try to process information quickly, often resulting in the formation of a label. With a label, the brain can bypass the effort it would take to really understand a person's unique perspective. Labels are often created by using a pattern-matching process to detect whether you trust, respect, like, dislike, or loathe a person, based on how accurately they match a pre-existing profile of a person you already know. How a person looks, sounds, even smells, can influence the label our brain associates to a newly encountered individual. This shortcut plays into another psychological phenomenon called *ingroup-outgroup bias* that all leaders need to be strongly aware of when trying to build a more inclusive environment.

Are You In? Then Reach Out...

Understanding the ingroup-outgroup bias and how to combat it may be the single most important thing you do to help humanity in your entire life. Let me explain. We can all agree that there are some individuals in our lives who are like us. They get us, they like us, they talk like us, wear the same clothes as us, and share many aspects in common with us. This typically results in favorable feelings toward these individuals because they resemble us in some form or fashion. The unfortunate reality is that we are more likely to provide special treatment, greater opportunities, and even more eye contact when communicating with these individuals than those who are different than us. This group of similar people is assigned as the ingroup. In the U.S., if you are Republican, you see other Republicans as the ingroup, and if you are a Democrat, you see other Democrats as the ingroup. The flag you wave with the capital *"R"* or capital "D" bonds you to a collective, which makes you feel connected. The problem, though, is by forming an ingroup, we automatically form an outgroup. An outgroup can be thought of as a group of people who hold alternative views, have different life experiences, or simply look different than those in the ingroup. Although ingroups and outgroups typically share far more in common (e.g. basic human needs, passion for their views, desire for improvement, etc.), it requires far less effort for the brain to point out the differences than it does the similarities between the groups. This is something all people—leaders included—are prone to do. To illustrate this point, imagine for a second, you are at a high-end sushi restaurant and you notice two different fish swimming in an aquarium across from you. Now that you have taken time to visualize the two fish, what do you notice? What are your first observations? Likely you will notice that one fish is larger than the other, perhaps one fish has more exotic colors than the other. Does one fish look more predatorial than the other? Maybe you notice that one fish has large scales while the other has smooth skin. My guess is the first thing that came to mind was not that both fish have gills, both are cold-blooded, and both are living in the same tank, yet these facts are just as available for your brain to process as the differences between the fish.

Unfortunately, history provides countless examples of persecution and scapegoating, resulting from rhetoric dividing ingroups from outgroups. When left to fester, the ingroup-outgroup bias leads to discrimination, hatred, and even genocide. Exaggerating the division between groups with propaganda has resulted in some of the most inhumane behaviors known to humanity. As a leader, you must understand how the ingroup-outgroup bias forms and continue to find ways to mitigate the negative impacts of this bias. Rising to power using hatred is much easier than rising to power with an inclusive mindset. Doing what's easy is not always doing what's right. You have a choice to make as a leader: create a culture of division using an *us vs. them* mentality, or create a culture of unity by embracing inclusion. If you desire the latter, then start considering how your thoughts and communications promote an ecosystem of inclusion, mutual understanding, and equality. Time and time again, we hear of tragedies (conflicts, shootings, suicides, etc.) that may have been prevented if people would have been willing to talk to those who appear different than themselves. Showing compassion and making the extra effort to understand those different from you can have a rippling effect on humanity.

Strengthen Bonds Across Group Lines

There is little question that you will experience ingroup and outgroup bias during your leadership journey. The question you need to ask yourself is, *how can I break the cycle within the teams I lead?* A famous psychological study conducted in 1958 by Mazufer Sherif found that when individuals belonging to opposing groups work towards a common goal, they can leave a situation with much more positive views of each other than before they started (Sherif, 1958). You have likely heard the expression, *"We've been through the trenches together"* throughout your career to describe a newly formed bond between people once belonging to conflicting groups. Serving in the military offers a great example of how people from all walks of life are able to put aside differences for a larger purpose. When immersed in a critical mission, it becomes quite clear that working together as a cohesive unit and having each other's back is far more important to success than a difference of opinion or background. When leading, seek opportunities to pair individuals on projects that will strengthen bonds across group lines. By doing so, each party will learn more about one another's perspective and together they will create a shared experience that will challenge their original assumptions. It's awfully hard for the brain to continue using a negative label for an entire outgroup when it just witnessed a member from that outgroup contribute to a shared goal in a positive way.

As important as it is to find opportunities for others to bridge differences, there is no better way to encourage inclusive behavior than to model it yourself. As a leader, you too need to proactively find those challenging opportunities to get out of your ingroup (e.g. attend an event where you are the minority, try to interact with someone who doesn't know your language, study other cultures willingly, etc.). Stop avoiding these types of opportunities out of fear it may get you out of your comfort zone. Stop seeking ways to confirm your existing beliefs—seek ways to challenge them. Confirming what we already believe is easy and comforting, but it is rarely conducive to promoting inclusion. Shift the fear you have of being challenged to a feeling of excitement in learning something new. This shift doesn't mean you have to agree with everything you hear, but at a minimum, you should be curious as to why certain individuals think and behave the way they do. Creating a greater understanding of others will help you find a greater understanding within yourself. Allow yourself to productively engage with those who hold differing views—they will open your eyes to new ideas and ways of thinking you would have otherwise missed out on. If you limit your interaction with members from outgroups, you will limit your ability to learn and apply lessons those individuals have already experienced. In my life, I have found there is no better way to accelerate development than possessing a willingness to see every person as having a unique story, one that can positively influence my own life. If you are willing to truly listen to others, you can exponentially increase your ability to acquire new knowledge. This perspective will help you make more inclusive decisions, ones that open doors for all to participate resulting in greater fairness and increase learning across the board.

Becoming more inclusive doesn't happen overnight; you will need to become more aware, tolerant, and willing to listen to others. When you do, two great opportunities will present themselves: the ability to see the world in a more encompassing light, and the ability to grow a stronger and more diverse network. The world is a large and beautifully diverse place. I encourage you to experience as much of it as you can, whether personally or vicariously.

 ## Lure #4: Curiosity
An ongoing desire to acquire new knowledge.

Curiosity didn't kill the cat; it was too busy consuming the minds of great leaders. Staying young at heart, this beautiful construct allows leaders to acquire limitless amounts of knowledge. Being curious is not childish, it's a vital part of leadership. Leaders should possess an ongoing desire to learn more so they can continually see the world differently. Given how much there is to explore in this world, (e.g. unique cultures, breathtaking sites, exotic foods to eat, interesting people to meet, etc.) every leader should be filled with excitement for the opportunities that lie ahead. The best part is all you have to do is be willing to ask the question.

Curiosity is simply an internal desire to learn something new. As a leader, being curious helps you attain new information, innovate new ways of working, and strengthens your ability to connect with others. Curious leaders don't settle for the status quo—they know that answers are out there for someone to find and who better to discover them but them. Craving the pursuit as much as they do the discovery, great leaders create an environment for others to think outside of the box and stay curious in an authentic manner.

Personally, I love it when my curiosity leads me to debunk false narratives I had previously believed. I know it sounds crazy, but there are times that I like being wrong. I love the *'Aha!'* moment that hits me like a ton of bricks when I realize what I previously believed was actually inaccurate, or only partially true. When this happens, I experience a mental paradigm shift that keeps me hungry to learn more. It's in this exact moment—the same moment many people fight so hard to avoid—that I truly feel young at heart and understand that I still have so much to learn. Some refer to this as the *learning paradox*—the more you learn, the more you realize how much more there is still left to learn. Instead of feeling inadequate or defeated with how much knowledge there is yet to learn in a given topic, feel proud that you expanded your horizons. Tomorrow will present itself with more opportunities to learn, as long as you foster it through your curiosity.

When I was in grad school, I had the amazing opportunity to go on my first international trip to Turkey. Turkey had always intrigued me as a curious child; I thought it was funny and somewhat confusing that the country shared the same name with the bird most Americans eat during Thanksgiving. This intrigue only grew on me as I saw those peculiar looking hats the Turks wore in the Indiana Jones films. As I grew older, I started learning more about the tremendous amount of history that took place in Turkey over the years—all of the wars, the changes of power, religion, and even city names (e.g. Constantinople to Istanbul). By the time I was in grad school, I was beyond ready to see what Turkey was all about. Now, I should also mention, that as eager as I was to experience something new, I was a little nervous about exploring foreign lands. Over the course of multiple decades, I had heard some not so flattering things about the country of Turkey. I heard stories of violence, crime, and the notoriously harsh prison system. I heard tales about weird Turkish bathhouses and how unsafe it could be to travel to a primarily Muslim country (even though at the time, Turkey was considered a secular state politically) as an American. But when push came to shove, I knew it was better to withhold judgment until I experienced Turkey first hand. After all how bad could it be and what better time to see a new part of the world upon finishing grad school?

Without going into great length about Turkey and all of the eye-opening experiences, I want to focus on three in particular that I still carry with me to this day:

1. Visiting a small community outside of Izmir and helping the Imam (priest) clean the community's Mosque. I vividly remember being in total awe walking up the stairs of the minbar, or pulpit, where prayers were led to dust the railings. This small community opened up their place for worship for me, a Westerner, to come in and better understand their faith and culture. They were so warm and inviting, even going out of their way to explain how the roots of Islam and Christianity originated from the same place.

2. Having an out of body experience at Hagia Sophia. This

building was simply magnificent. Walking through the exhibits, I was overcome by all kinds of intense emotions and stimuli. The structure served as a church for the Byzantines (Christians) and was transformed into a mosque when the Ottomans took over the city in 1453. The Ottomans saw the beauty and mystique of the structure and decided not to tear it down even though it was the place for worship of their enemies.

3. Forming a connection with the symbol of the *Nazar* and its protection from the *evil eye*. You have likely seen this symbol—whether hanging from the rear-view mirror in a car or on a piece of jewelry. It's usually a blue circular object, made out of glass or porcelain, with a single eye in the center. It serves as protection from the judgmental eye we receive from others. Every time I see the symbol now, I make sure to ask the individual who possesses it a question related to Turkey or the Middle East. This connection prompts me to interact with someone I likely would not have otherwise approached.

These experiences, along with many others, have helped shape my understanding of the world. Through my own curiosity, I have challenged pre-existing labels which have led me to see the world in an entirely different light. As a leader, it can be easy to make decisions based on the labels others give, but building a leadership legacy isn't about doing what's easy—it's about digging deeper, even when others have already passed judgment. Seek to find a unique story in each and every person you meet. Consider the possibility that every person has a perspective that can help you become a better leader—whether you initially agree with them or not. No one country, philosophy, or tribe of like-minded people has all of the challenges that pain humanity figured out, but what if you could extract the greatest elements of each through your ongoing curiosity?

Extract The Best Elements Of Humanity Through Your Curiosity

A corporate example of how curiosity benefits leaders was revealed to me a few years back when I had the chance to interview a leader from a Fortune 100 company. I was very intrigued by how this particular leader built his high performing teams. He told me that he proactively sought out individuals that others had passed over or given negative labels to. Instead of going with the crowd and looking to build teams the way other leaders did, in his words— *"Looking for the same alpha dogs that currently held leadership positions"*—he would prioritize time to learn about the different skills and values people of all backgrounds could bring to his team. He said that once he was able to understand peoples' backgrounds, personal stories, and the type of work they excelled at, he was able to easily recruit them (since other leaders had labeled and passed over them) to his team. He said that by believing in them and giving them a sense of purpose, he was able to *"untap"* hidden potential others were not curious enough to discover for themselves. It helped diversify his team and provided him with new knowledge and experiences to increase his effectiveness as a leader. Additionally, it empowered the people he recruited to redefine themselves and combat false labels. When organizations solely focus on recruiting for a single type or label of people, they do themselves a huge disservice. It takes a curious leader to ask why, and dig deeper into the precise skills, values, and motivations that produce the best teams.

Possessing an ongoing desire to acquire new knowledge as a leader is like fishing from a lake with endless opportunities. Instead of regularly fishing the same waters that limit yourself, let others' uniqueness propel your boat through new waters. Let new ideas challenge and enlighten you. Keep asking questions, because if you aren't curious about others, others will never be curious about you.

Lure #5: Diversity of Thought

Proactively seeking out new ideas and perspectives to improve one's overall understanding.

In life, you find what you seek. Your thoughts paint not only your realities but also the information you use to confirm them. Holding onto any kind of inclination will influence the way you search for information. If you believe that attending a leadership conference will help you develop as a leader, chances are you will find evidence at the conference that supports your original position. If you attend the same conference but believe you will learn nothing that you didn't already know, chances are you will find evidence to support that claim as well. The reason we tend to find what we seek is due to a psychological phenomenon known as *confirmation bias*. Confirmation bias refers to our tendency to seek out information that supports our initial thoughts or expectations disproportionately more than seeking information that contradicts it. Think about the choices you make in terms of how you source your information in life. What news network do you tend to find yourself watching the most? Which influencers do you follow regularly? Which podcasts do you listen to? What is it about these specific outlets that keep you coming back? An even better question is how often do you seek an alternative perspective from these preferred sources?

If you are like most people, you probably tend to watch media and listen to others who hold similar views to you. By doing so, you confirm your beliefs and don't have to experience that uncomfortable mental state known as *cognitive dissonance*, which I will discuss in greater detail next chapter. But in the meantime ask yourself this, how effective is it to only consume one angle of every argument all the time? If there are at least three sides to every story (yours, mine, and the truth), why do people prefer to only hear the side that coincides with the narrative they want to hear? Leadership is not about listening to the stories you want to hear, but rather, seeking out the stories you don't want to hear. Not only does confirmation bias limit the overall knowledge you can gain, but it can also negatively influence your interactions and relationships, leaving you with a very bland and one-sided worldview. It's so important to make a conscious effort to interact with people who can keep you honest and provide alternative perspectives.

Keep An Open Mind—Seek Out The Stories You Are Not Inclined To Hear

A few years ago, I was at an orientation training in Orlando with a number of new hires for the large consulting firm I worked for. I remember very clearly that I didn't know anyone else at the event which hosted 300-400 new hires in total. After breakfast on the first day, I reported to my homeroom where 30 or so of us sat around circle tables awaiting instructions. Very early on in the session, I noticed a young man, similar to me in age, with a distinct Australian accent, who was actively participating and seemed to know what the hell he was talking about. Here I was just trying not to look stupid in front of my peers and this Aussie was getting all of the attention from the room. I remember my initial thought was, *Oh boy, here we go again with another young, ambitious, smart professional with a foreign accent who is going to be the darling of the session.* At first, I remembered harboring resentment toward him, and telling myself that he was probably a silver-spoon-fed brat whose rich parents paid for his education and travels to the U.S. I started confirming this belief by looking for cues, like the suit and shoes he was wearing, and the way he interacted with what appeared to be a number of friends he had already made at the event. Clearly, I was out of my comfort zone and needed to construct this narrative to help justify my own insecurities and negativity. To this day (or until he reads this book), this poor lad had no idea what my original judgments were of him. If he did at the time, he probably wouldn't be the dear friend he is to me now. The Aussie's name was Jack, and our acquaintance soon turned into a deep friendship shortly after the first session. The turning point was being paired with Jack at the second session where we worked on a business case together. It turned out that later that night, we both saw each other working out at the gym, and Jack happened to be wearing a San Diego Padres hat—the same city that I had just moved to. I started thinking to myself, *Maybe I was completely wrong, what if Jack was actually more like me than I could have ever imagined?* The next day we sat by each other during breakfast, and he shared with me that he transferred from the Australia office and had been working in Sacramento, CA. He went on to tell me how he had visited San Diego and absolutely loved it. He also shared how he had come from a similar middle class and modest family just like myself. At the conclusion of breakfast, we agreed that we would meet up for dinner and drinks that evening with some other colleagues, and that is exactly what we did. Now, I'm not sure what your experiences have been going out with Aussies, but mine usually all end the same way—feeling like I got hit by a bus the next morning. Needless to say, Jack and I had a blast that night, requiring us to stay plenty hydrated with water the next morning. At breakfast, we laughed as we caught up on all the shenanigans from the night before. We ended up exchanging numbers that morning and Jack told me he wanted to meet up the next time he was in San Diego. Well, sure enough, about a year later, Jack and his fiancée came out to San Diego and we met up. After a toast to both of their well-deserved promotions, Jack inquired how my book was coming along. He was so sincere in wanting to know more about the premise and progress that it gave me a tremendous amount of inspiration to keep going. He even offered to volunteer to help proof and edit a draft version. After that night, I made a mental note to write this section, because I was wrong about Jack. Here, a man I was ready to write off and let my own confirmation bias find all the reasons why I shouldn't like, gave me the great gifts of self-assurance and ongoing support. It was the real confirmation I needed to know that this book could resonate with other aspiring leaders like Jack.

Now you may be thinking, *This is great information and a light-hearted story, but what practical steps can I take to mitigate the dangers of confirmation bias on my own leadership journey?* Knowing that it's not possible, or practical, to obtain every viewpoint from every person on the planet, you must make a conscious effort to balance the sources of information you consume. Additionally, you need to take a good look at how you are currently prioritizing your time in terms of the interactions you have throughout the day.

There is no doubt that in today's digital age, it's crucial for leaders to prioritize their time. This same principle also holds true when deciding the types of people you surround yourself with on your leadership journey. Let's face it, as much as we may want to interact with everyone we come across, it may not always be practical or productive for our development. All the commitments you have (family, friends, work, finances, hobbies, etc.) require a proactive mindset when it comes to attracting the right leaders to groom. So, how should you determine who gets invited to go fishing on your boat?

In Addition To Prioritizing Tasks, Prioritize Your Interactions

You may be familiar with Stephen Covey's Time Management Matrix, the model that helps individuals decide which tasks to prioritize in their busy day. Covey outlines how we should think of the tasks we need to complete by examining two continuums: *how urgent the task is* and *how important it is*. Categorizing tasks based on these two continuums allows for individuals to prioritize important/urgent tasks over non-important/non-urgent tasks (Covey, 2004).

Taking a page from Covey's playbook, it dawned on me that leaders in today's digital world may need help prioritizing the relationships that will be most meaningful to their legacy. Instead of thinking about tasks, start thinking about how you prioritize your leadership interactions. If your goal is to be a great leader by developing others while simultaneously developing yourself, start prioritizing your interactions using the *Catching Leadership Interaction Matrix* on the following page.

CATCHING LEADERSHIP INTERACTION MATRIX

To prioritize your leadership interactions, consider two continuums: *diversity* and *motivation to lead*. When you think of diversity, it goes beyond race, color, or creed—think of the leadership skills, experiences, and ideas an individual has that may be similar to or different from your own. By prioritizing individuals who are different than you, you will increase the amount of new knowledge you can share, as well as the new knowledge you can learn. Secondly, ask yourself if the individual is motivated to be a leader. If there is no motivation to lead, there will be little you can do to help an individual become a better leader; therefore, you will be better served to prioritize your time with those who want to lead *vs.* those who do not.

When it comes to prioritizing your leadership interactions, remember this fishing metaphor: when deciding who to take fishing on your boat, invite a partner who sincerely wants to fish and brings a unique tackle box to complement your own. In other words, attract *anglers* (motivated to lead) over *spectators* (not motivated to lead) and individuals who bring unique skills/experiences (diverse) over those who share the same skills/experiences as you (not diverse). To unpack this further, think of some of the individuals who fall into each of these four categories in your life.

	DIVERSE	NOT DIVERSE
MOTIVATED	(1) Diverse Anglers	(2) Familiar Anglers
NOT MOTIVATED	(3) Diverse Spectators	(4) Familiar Spectators

1) **Diverse Anglers** - Diverse individuals who possess a great desire to lead. They possess unique skills, experiences, and ideas different from your own. They provide you with new perspectives and ideas that will challenge your own worldview. In return, you provide them the same, which enhances their own leadership journey.

2) **Familiar Anglers** - Individuals who are similar to you, yet also possess a great desire to lead. You will likely be able to build relationships with them quickly and help them fine-tune the skills you have in common. They will reinforce your perspective (for better or worse) but offer little insight into new ways of thinking.

3) **Diverse Spectators** - Diverse individuals who possess no desire to lead. They provide you with unique ideas and experiences but enter your boat without the intention to cast a line. What you learn from your interactions with them may help you relate to future anglers down the road, but interactions with this group should not be prioritized over anglers who are ready to cast their own lines.

4) **Familiar Spectators** - Individuals similar to you who have no desire to lead. These individuals won't offer you much in terms of new knowledge or perspective. You will likely enjoy their company, and they yours, but instead of catching leadership on your boat, they are likely more interested in catching a buzz.

When it comes to leadership development, you will greatly benefit by prioritizing the interactions on your boat in this order:
1). **Diverse Anglers**
2). **Familiar Anglers**
3). **Diverse Spectators**
4). **Familiar Spectators**

That is, of course, if your goal is to continue your own development while developing other leaders. If your goal is to relax and go fishing with your drinking buddy, you know who to call up.

This model makes it seem easy, but fishing with someone who fishes a different style or technique is uncomfortable—but that's the point! You both will benefit by pushing yourselves outside of your comfort zones and will learn a tremendous amount in the process. The beauty is that the more you learn, the more you will want to keep learning from others. By prioritizing these types of interactions, you and your first mate will both be better positioned to weather the inevitable storms leadership will bring.

It's not rocket science to conclude that fishing the same lures, in the same spots, with the same people, yields the same developmental results. If you are ready to take your leadership development to the next level, it's time to break the mold and put yourself out there. It's time to *Attract Diverse Anglers.*

CHAPTER 3

Tie Their Knot

Set Aside Personal Ambition for Mutual Long-Term Success

"Give a man a fish and you feed him for a day. Teach a man to fish and you feed him for a lifetime."

−UNKNOWN

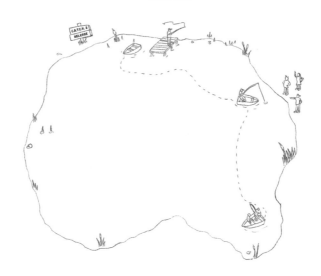

Leadership Constructs Discussed in *Tie Their Knot*
Strategic Outlook • Delayed Gratification • Passion to Enlighten

"What a Beauty!" I said, netting Bob's four-and-a-half-pound smallie. His catch was just what we needed to warm our dampened spirits that chilly morning. After unhooking the fish and placing it into the livewell, we gave each other a big high five. Getting in on the celebration, our boat driver said, *"See, I told you they're in here!"* As Bob was getting re-situated, I remember asking every detail about his bite, the color of his lure, and how the fish took it. Working as part of a team, Bob had no problem sharing all he could remember right before his rod tip took a nosedive. I specifically remember asking him for a tube bait in the same smoke color (purplish grey) so I could match his rig exactly. *"You're using a Palomar knot, right?"* I asked as Bob confirmed with a nod. Not being familiar with the dead sticking technique, I needed to ensure I had a presentable lure and secure knot in order to confidently cast my line. With new-found hope, I threw my lure out over a rock pile and waited for my opportunity to shine.

Do you remember the first time you went fishing? Perhaps it was when you were younger, or maybe it happened more recently. Regardless of when it happened, chances are, you probably don't remember the clothes you were wearing, how the weather was, or whether or not you even caught a fish. There is one question I bet you can answer about that day though: Who tied your knot? Was it a family member, a close friend, or perhaps a fishing guide? It probably wasn't you, and whoever it was, I bet they were intentional in their method to set you up for success. Taking a moment to put down their pole, they invested time and energy into tying a knot that would initiate your fishing journey. As a leader, you will undoubtedly have similar opportunities to tie the knots of others. When asked, what will you do? Complain, continue fishing for yourself, or create a mutual experience that leaves a life-lasting impression on another individual?

Whether you're an avid angler or not, we *all* tie knots. From the time we first learn to tie our shoes to the time we say, *"I do,"* knots are used both literally and metaphorically to connect the loose ends of our lives.

Rehearsing the same series of steps time and time again we gain confidence in securing knots we know we can count. Before long, these knot tying behaviors become somewhat mindless until someone or something helps us once again see our knots from a whole new perspective.

The insights gained when asked to slow down and explain each step that goes into tying the knots we regularly tie in our own lives is truly amazing. When we instruct others, it forces us to pump the brakes and see the world from the lens of a novice. This process teaches us a number of valuable leadership lessons: patience, empathy, and learning how to communicate at a more basic level. The process not only allows for the transfer of knowledge, but it also reminds us where we, too, once came from.

Tying Knots For Others Reminds Us Where We Once Came From

Consider this change in perspective the next time you are asked to help a young child tie their necktie. You could tie it for them, putting the tie around your own neck and going through the same motions you always do. Once you have tied a beautiful knot, you could simply slip the tie off your own head and put it over their head for them to tighten. This will solve the immediate problem and leave them satisfied for a day, but if you take the time to teach them how to do it themselves, you will have made an impression lasting a lifetime.

As a child, I recall several memories fishing with my father. He, like many fathers, was pretty excited about the idea of catching fish with his new little fishing buddy. He bought me my first pole, which I still remember to this day. It was a two-foot rod, with a yellow and white reel, and a decal of *Snoopy* (the Peanuts cartoon character) on the side. The night before we went fishing, Dad always made sure to organize his tackle box, check the forecast, and tie on the lures we planned to use first. We would have fun giving the lures nicknames and trying to predict which colors would produce the best results. He always went the extra mile to make sure we had everything we needed for a fun evening of fishing, including the mosquito repellent for those Iowa summer nights.

Today, I fully understand and appreciate the time and commitment Dad made for my brothers and me to have great fishing experiences. He worked hard, not only during his day job in a metal factory but also when he got home, to make sure his kids could enjoy the same activities that he did. His dedication and work ethic didn't stop when we got to the water—in fact, it must have felt like it was just beginning.

There is little doubt in my mind that my dad's top priority those first few trips was to teach me how to fish, but I also know he had a desire to catch fish himself. It was a sport in which he had developed a unique skill set and passion for. I imagine he anticipated spending some time, but not the majority of his time, teaching me how to tie a knot, cast my line, untangle twists out of my reel, etc. But... that's exactly what he spent the majority of his time doing in those early years. Needless to say, after several snags, bug bites, and hours of boredom, I was usually ready to leave before my dad could even get into a rhythm of properly fishing an area. Dad never complained (well, at least not very much), and he was always willing to put aside his own aspirations of catching fish to show me what fishing was all about.

When fishing with less experienced anglers, everything—and I mean everything—seems to require a little more effort, a little more explanation, and a lot more patience. Whatever can go wrong typically does, and there is definitely no guarantee that either of you will even catch any fish. The bottom line is this: if my dad wouldn't have tied my first knot, I never would have become a passionate angler, I would have never joined the University of Iowa Bass fishing team, and I would have never authored this book.

The 3rd step of the *C.A.T.C.H. & Release* Model, *Tie Their Knot*, requires a mental shift, one that prioritizes the development of others over the self-interests of oneself. During this shift, a leader begins valuing the enlightening of others equally, if not greater than, achieving personal results. At first, this change may result in *cognitive dissonance* or a mental state of discomfort resulting when a person's actions do not align with their existing attitudes or beliefs. This psychological concept is not new, in fact, cognitive dissonance was coined over a half-century ago by the University of Iowa graduate, Leon Festinger (Festinger, 1957). Don't be fooled by the publication date though—as a leader your ability to fully understand the elements of cognitive dissonance is just as important today as it was back in the 1950s. To illustrate this concept further consider the following scenario.

A FISHING DILEMMA

On a sunny Autumn morning, you find yourself fishing from your boat with an inexperienced angler. This innocent angler means well but is having the most difficult time with some of the most basic fishing tasks. You can tell that their confidence is waning as your co-angler starts to question their own abilities. Your day has been relatively slow with just a few little bites, yet you know first hand that big fish do reside in this lake because the last time you fished it an absolute giant broke off your line. Trying to get your redemption today, you suddenly hear a loud *Spooooooolsh* as a huge fish jumps out of the water about ten yards in front of your boat. *I BET that's the big one that got away last time*, you think to yourself. As your heart races, you quickly position the boat for a casting opportunity in the direction of the jump. With daylight starting to fade and not much to show in terms of your boat's productivity, you feel a sense of urgency to catch this fish. You have been telling friends and colleagues for weeks that this trip would be the one you finally land your trophy. With winter right around the corner, and the fishing season dwindling, you convince yourself that this is your last chance to catch a quality fish this year.

Quietly, you bring the boat to a gentle stop in the perfect casting position. As you do so you are reminded of the new angler you bought along sitting next to you. Eager to soak in as much knowledge as possible and show you they can fish, is having one hell of a time keeping their line untangled and lure in the strike zone. Over the last few hours you have seen a change in your partner's body language and get a sense that they are losing hope. This type of fishing is new to them, but regardless of the setbacks, the new angler has expressed how grateful they are to have someone like you there to guide them. Even though the day has not been ideal, you have enjoyed their company. To your surprise, you have even learned a thing or two listening to them tell their fishing stories. In addition to listening, you have also started opening up, sharing some of your own fishing stories and secrets. A really big part of you wants to make a lasting impression on this new angler and end the day with a bang. It crosses your mind that the best way to do just that is hooking into a trophy fish right in front of them.

Softly reaching over to grab your best fishing rod, you realize you have an identical lure to the one you hooked into the big one last time. As you loosen some line and wind up to make your cast, you hear your fellow angler abruptly say, "*Sorry... but my line broke again, can you tie a new knot for me, or should I just give up...*"

In this moment, you have a choice to make. On one hand, tying the knot may cost you precious minutes, which could result in a missed opportunity to land the prized fish that just jumped out of the water. On the other hand, if you decide not to tie the knot, the new angler may give up all hope in despair, missing their own shot at catching the trophy and perhaps never fishing again—at least the technique you have been trying so hard to teach them today. There is a strong part of you that really wants to land this fish yourself allowing you to finally prove to all your coworkers how great of an angler you are; but, there is another part of you that recognizes this as a golden leadership moment: a chance to role-model something the new angler may never forget.

A Fishing Dilemma

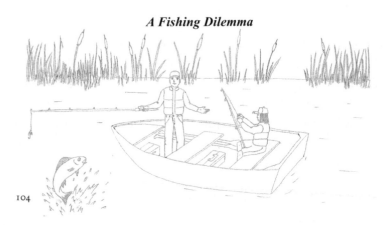

So, what do you do? Regardless of the decision you make, you can count on experiencing cognitive dissonance if the action you take does not align with your internal beliefs. In other words, whatever decision you make, you need to fully own and accept that action as part of a greater set of values or beliefs in order to alleviate mental discomfort. If your initial intention was to take the new angler out on the water to help improve their skill set, but in the heat of the moment you decide to choose your own personal excitement over theirs, you may feel guilty later on down the road. If your intention from the onset was to catch a trophy fish, and you brought the new angler along as a courtesy, you will be kicking yourself if you miss your perfect opportunity to finally catch the one that got away.

This dilemma illustrates the power of understanding your priorities upfront and being intentional as a leader. If you are not strategic or intentional, any fish that jumps out of the water (i.e. new project, email, or meeting invite that hits your inbox) will serve as an excuse to avoid taking the time to tie a new angler's knot. The level of cognitive dissonance you experience during any leadership dilemma will always depend on how aligned the action you take is to your existing attitudes and beliefs. Note that if you regularly find yourself needing to rationalize your behavior (e.g. *but it's just this one time…* or *everyone else does it why shouldn't I…*) to remove unnecessary mental strain, there is likely an opportunity for you to strengthen your knot tying ability as a leader.

On your leadership journey, it is important to proactively remind yourself what your long-term vision and goals are. A great way to do this is revisiting your leadership statement outlined in the introduction with regularity. Failing to fully understand your vision and core values will make you much more prone to reactive decision-making, ultimately leading to unintended or negative leadership consequences. Using the fishing dilemma I just described, let's consider some of the pros and cons of deciding to, and not to tie the new angler's knot.

| Deciding NOT TO tie a new angler's knot ||
Pros	Cons
Requires less effort upfront	A failed opportunity to role model leadership
Greater probability of personal success	Bottlenecks the development of others
There will be an immediate outcome	Risk being labeled a self-interested leader

On the pro-side, deciding not to tie the knot requires less personal effort, allowing you to focus more energy on your individual goal of catching the trophy fish. It provides short-term peace of mind (regardless of the outcome) because you know you were able to give your all trying to achieve a personal want. If you are successful, in the short-term, you will experience great satisfaction and likely recognition from others.

On the con-side, your action not to tie the knot serves as an example to others that you prioritize personal success over collective success. Caught up in the excitement of the moment, you may have missed a strategic opportunity to share a lasting experience with a new angler. This missed opportunity may have hindered the ability for the new angler to pay forward your gesture (teaching others how to tie the knots in high-pressure situations). Lastly, deciding not to tie the knot doesn't guarantee imminent success. While you may have eliminated the 'what if' question in your mind in the short-term, it may come full circle later in your career when you begin reflecting on your legacy as a leader. At some point or another, you will reflect back on the number of lives you were able to impact and the knowledge you were able to transfer. You may experience some level of regret if those quick casts you made trying to secure personal glory inhibited you from teaching others skills they could use for the rest of their lives.

| Deciding TO tie a new angler's knot ||
Pros	Cons
Creates mutual opportunities for success	Requires patience and self-control
Serves as a valuable teaching opportunity	Can be emotionally laboring
Prioritizes long-term rewards over short	Securing an immediate reward may be at risk

There never seems to be an ideal time to tie a new angler's knot. Balancing the developmental needs of others against your own personal ambitions is a difficult skill to master. It requires self-control, a strategic outlook, and a passion to enlighten others. It's crucial that leaders are able to recognize the difference between activities that are aligned to mutual long-term goals *vs.* self-interested ones that can produce a false sense of accomplishment in the here and now. If you have decided that developing others is pivotal to your own success as a leader, then taking the time to tie knots is critical in fulfilling your mission. Over time, envision all the knots you tie for others as culminating into a giant leadership net that will catch countless experiences, relationships, and lasting memories making up your legacy.

Revisiting the fishing dilemma, the pros of tying a new angler's knot are that you role model the importance of prioritizing mutual goals over self-interested goals. You plant the seeds for long-term growth—which is one of the greatest gifts any human can make for another. You remove any future guilt you may have experienced down the road had you caught the fish for yourself because you allowed a new angler to equally participate in the process. Lastly, you create a positive and reciprocal experience that is not dependent on catching a fish, you make it a win-win through your passion to enlighten another.

Of course, there is a flip side if you decide to tie the knot. It will likely generate thoughts of missed opportunities and decreased productivity. It may make you more irritable or even downright frustrated, feeling like you are just wasting time teaching someone else when it would be faster to just catch the fish yourself. At some point in the process, you may start to question why you agreed to decide to tie their knot in the first place—especially true when progress is slow at first. You may begin to entertain thoughts like, *life is too short, why should I sacrifice my opportunity at greatness just to help another noobie?* This thinking, as flawed as it may be, occurs naturally when torn between competing priorities; however, this logic is flawed because it assumes that you can only have one or the other.

Just because you take the time to tie another person's knot doesn't mean you forego the opportunity to catch the fish you've been intending to catch yourself. It might not look exactly the way it did initially in your mind, but it's still possible to have the best of both worlds. What if you were still able to catch that same fish *after* you tied their knot? By prescribing to the mindset that you can have both, you allow yourself a shot at personal redemption in catching the big fish while also having a companion there to help celebrate it with you. Even better, what if the new angler happens to catch the trophy fish from the knot you just tied? The decision to tie it then not only brings you joy and a sense of personal satisfaction, but it also creates a life-long memory for the new angler. Their excitement and new-found belief in the style of fishing you taught them will propel them to come back to the water time and time again. As the new angler reflects on your actions that day, they may be more inclined to pay it forward, tying the knots of other future leaders. For you, the *big fish that got away* story now has the perfect ending, and you have a co-angler who will carry on your legend through their own catch.

Let's explore how tying a new leader's knot may unfold in a more traditional work setting. A while back, I had the chance to work on a project engaging with a group of senior leaders from a technology company that was growing rapidly. One leader, in particular, stood out to me. She had worked at the organization nearly her entire career and found herself in a strategic role, reporting to the highest leaders in the organization.

After a few interactions with this leader, I started picking up on some behavioral patterns. She was well versed when it came to the operations of the organization and clearly understood how work got done within the company. She was perceived by others as a go-getter because she always appeared to be extremely busy. She was notorious for working a ridiculous number of hours and sending emails after midnight. When it came to explaining things that she already knew to others, she had a difficult time exhibiting patience. You could always tell her mind was somewhere else, worrying about what else needed to get done or what other deadline was in jeopardy of being missed. Does this person sound like anyone you may know?

To the credit of this leader, she had risen through the ranks thanks to her incredible drive and skill set to manage large-scale projects. Despite having robust technical acumen and the know-how to get things done, she didn't necessarily climb the ladder based on her ability to lead others (a common pitfall in many organizations). Now finding herself in a new leadership position, she struggled at times to strategically lead others. My personal interactions with this leader seemed to follow a very similar pattern. The first few minutes of conversation were spent with me listening to all of the chaotic things that were going on in the department, followed by how the night before she was up until midnight working on emails and putting out fires. Only after I acknowledged that she had a lot going on could we truly get down to the matter at hand, which was still interrupted several times by long pauses of her checking her phone and laptop. I can't say for sure, but my hunch was that she conditioned herself to believe that not being *busy* all the time equated to being stupid, lazy, or even worse—unproductive.

Her M.O. had become so reactive that she missed golden opportunities to properly train her direct reports. There was one direct report in particular who would follow her around, trying to learn as much as he could. He was hungry to gain more leadership experience but kept getting sucked into the reactive world his manager lived in. To no surprise, over the course of several months, her direct report decided to leave the organization to pursue other endeavors. From what I observed, some of the contributing factors were: lack of development opportunities, the unsustainable role of playing firefighter all day, and a lack of authenticity from his leader maintaining the *I am so busy* facade. All of these reactive behaviors resulted in the direct report being deprived of meaningful feedback and proactive coaching on how best to develop his own leadership abilities.

Being Busy For Busy Sake Limits Growth

Take a second to reflect on your own behaviors. Maybe you have been in a similar situation yourself. Perhaps a new colleague needs support with a task, but instead of taking the time to train them upfront, you offer to complete the task yourself because it will require less time and effort. Knowing this is unsustainable and that your colleague will likely ask you to complete the same task for them again in the future, why do you procrastinate the inevitable? Instead, take a more strategic viewpoint and begin to see the time and energy upfront as an investment that will pay greater dividends down the road. If you fail to learn this important leadership lesson you will cap your potential prematurely due to your inability to scale. For this reason, it is so important to check in with yourself throughout the course of the day, especially when you are feeling completely swamped, to make sure you are prioritizing your activities with the long-term in mind. Upon retirement or death, for that matter, will anyone know or care about the 1,567,327 emails you sent during your career? Will they write on your gravestone, *"Never missed a meeting"* or *"Responded to every text message within 30 seconds?"* When that final curtain drops, you will be remembered by the lasting impressions you made on those who needed you the most. Accept that there will always be administrative tasks to fulfill within your role, but don't let those mundane tasks blind you from the bigger picture. It's time to break the short-term cycle that inhibits all parties (the leader, the learner, and the organization) and start welcoming chances to *Tie Their Knot*.

THE KNOTS OF LEADERSHIP

Think of tying others' knots as synonymous with onboarding the next generation of leaders. Effective onboarding can positively influence an individual's engagement and tenure. It's for these very reasons that many organizations invest substantial resources to ensure new employees are set up with the knowledge and skills needed to hit the ground running. Organizations that fail to do so run the grave risk of losing high-potentials, especially millennials, who prefer working for leaders who make time to tie their knots. As a leader, I encourage you to listen to your new hires' long-term goals and stretch them with assignments aligned to those long-term goals. Show—through your actions—that you value learning opportunities over *busywork*. A core responsibility of any leader is to onboard others with the knowledge and skills they need to succeed. Regardless of whether or not you had to *'learn it the hard way'*, it's your obligation to pay forward your knowledge. Remember that you serve as the gatekeeper to a new leader's potential. If you are unwilling to set your own rod down momentarily in order to enable others to start casting, you serve as a bottleneck in their development. The art to tying better knots is possessing a strategic outlook (being *proactive* over *reactive*), delaying gratification (prioritizing *self-control* over *self-indulgence*), and a passion to enlighten (*sharing knowledge* over *withholding knowledge*).

Knot #1: Strategic Outlook
The ability to keep a long-term strategy in mind during day-to-day activities.

Throughout the course of a day, leaders face hundreds, if not thousands, of distractions. Even right now, as you read this, there are likely two or three other things on your mind that have nothing to do with your own development, not to mention the notification that just went off on your phone. In today's world, we are bombarded with constant distractions. While technology connects us to the world in more ways than ever, it often comes with the price of mindless scrolling online and a feeling of FOMO (fear of missing out). Not all distractions are bad—some distractions keep us safe—such as a severe weather alert or an ambulance on the road requiring us to slow down and pull over. However, the vast majority of distractions provide little value on one's leadership journey. In fact, they hinder a person's ability to focus on what matters most. Every time you react to a distraction, you reallocate mental and physical resources toward something new. This is problematic on two fronts: 1.) There is only so much energy you can expend in a day. In order to achieve your long-term goals, you have to prioritize your energy on activities that will progress you toward your desired end state. 2.) The brain is not very effective at multitasking—at least not in the way most people think of multitasking. While it's true the brain interprets and sends countless signals every second (subconsciously), it has a difficult time performing conscious tasks effectively at the same time.

Knowing this, and the fact that distractions will always exist, wouldn't it be more meaningful as a leader to proactively plan and stick to the activities that are aligned to your long-term goals? Throughout your day, ask yourself, *What am I doing right now?* Then follow that question with another question, *How is this action helping me achieve what it is I have set out to achieve?* If you can't answer the second question in a way that makes you feel good about the action, likely you are simply reacting to a distraction. To be clear, I am not recommending that you stop responding to your emails because they don't all align perfectly with your leadership statement. What I *am* saying is try to make a conscious effort to be intentional about the activities you do partake in. Not every single email, text message, or squirrel you see out the window requires immediate attention. Be strategic. Set parameters for yourself and keep them. You are in the driver's seat of your life, don't let distractions from the back seat dictate where you drive the car.

Knot #2: Delayed Gratification

The ability to postpone immediate rewards in exchange for greater long-term rewards.

Patience. The skill most people will answer when asked what fishing has taught them about life. All leaders need to exhibit a degree of patience within themselves, especially when working with others. Patience, in a lot of ways, can be viewed as a type of sacrifice—the ability to decline something now for something greater in the future.

Think about a time when you had to sacrifice something you really enjoyed. A time when you really had to exhibit self-control to the nth degree. What did you learn about yourself during that experience? My guess is at first you hated the idea of refraining from whatever it was you were giving up, likely thinking of all the reasons why it was stupid to have to give it up in the first place. Did you ever think to yourself that *life is short, tomorrow I may get hit by a bus, I might as well enjoy all of the pleasures of life right here and now?* After feeling sorry for yourself, perhaps even throwing a tizzy or two, something inside of you eventually shifted. Instead of victimizing yourself and rationalizing short-term pleasures, you started to feel proud of the fact that you were exhibiting some self-control. While the temptation remained constant, you were less affected by the initial craving and began to feel empowered by the progress you were making. Once you hit this tipping point, you began to see and feel the benefits of the self-control you exhibited. Your thoughts changed from *life's short, why shouldn't I?* to *I'm so glad I kept that commitment I made to myself!*

As you begin thinking about your own experiences with delayed gratification, what common examples come to mind? A new diet? Your desire to quit an addiction? A specific financial goal? Typically, when we think about self-control or delaying short-term rewards for greater long-term ones, we think of things we *"give up"* or *"cut out"* of our life, but have you ever thought about this same concept through the lens of leadership? Being an effective leader requires an ability to differentiate the actions that provide immediate pleasure (e.g. making an impulsive decision, bending the rules for yourself, avoiding a difficult conversation, etc.) which tend to result in detrimental long-term consequences (e.g. career stagnation, losing the trust of an employee, or even a tarnished reputation) from those that do not. As a leader, there will be many times that you must exhibit self-control over your own personal ambitions for the greater long-term good of the team. Will you be open to these opportunities? For example, let's say you have a weekly meeting during which you get to present to the senior leaders in your organization. Are you comfortable allowing someone else on your team to use that opportunity to develop their skills, even if it means he or she won't deliver the presentation exactly the way you would? In the short-term, you may be sacrificing immediate recognition from senior leaders; yet, in the long-term, you may have just provided a future leader with invaluable leadership experience and a lesson on how to share opportunities as a leader. Throughout your day, there are likely several instances (e.g. postponing scheduled meetings, failing to speak up, keeping your office door closed) that may feel good in the short-term, but ultimately impede your ability to be the most effective leader you can be in the long-term. My advice to you is to strive for a better balance between your personal needs and the needs of others. Ask yourself frequently, *does the short-term gain of this decision help or hurt my overall goal of being a great leader?* What will provide you with a greater sense of satisfaction later in life: personally catching the fish that just jumped out of the water, or knowing that you tied the knots of countless leaders who now have the opportunity to do the same?

Knot #3: Passion to Enlighten

Experiencing a great sense of fulfillment when educating others.

Knowledge is one of the greatest gifts any leader receives throughout their lives. It provides a fresh perspective, unlocks new opportunities, and can be shared exponentially. Knowledge *is* power, and the most powerful leaders have a knack for both acquiring it and sharing it with others.

It's fair to say that not every leader approaches knowledge with the same mindset. Some leaders fall into the trap of viewing knowledge as a finite and stagnant resource. By finite, I mean there is *only so much knowledge*, and by stagnant, I mean that *knowledge never changes.* Leaders who view knowledge this way hoard it because they think it gives them an edge over others. Prescribing to this notion is detrimental to their leadership ability in a number of ways. First, information and knowledge are always changing based on new research and evidence. Trying to hold onto secret knowledge is a futile effort because of how quickly new information is acquired and shared in the digital age. Leaders who try to hoard information to themselves in order to maintain the *smartest person in the room* image will soon find themselves in an empty room, or worse, in a room full of ignorance. Great leaders aren't afraid of surrounding themselves with teams who are smarter than they are; instead, they encourage it. If knowledge *is* power, the question then becomes, how can a leader become most powerful? The answer: openly sharing knowledge to create an environment where the best ideas prevail.

Great Leaders Surround Themselves With Teams Who Are Smarter Than They Are

A passion for enlightening others is not something that comes easy for most people. It takes patience and an even deeper understanding of a topic than mere comprehension. Teaching any subject requires breaking down concepts into more consumable parts that allow others to make their own connections. To do this effectively, you have to know the content (or knowledge) in great detail and prepare a delivery that will resonate with the audience. For some leaders, this requires too much effort. They would rather take on additional work, or make excuses in order to avoid the opportunity to enlighten another. Great leaders, however, don't avoid opportunities to enlighten others—they live for those moments. When the light bulb goes off, and a smile of understanding is displayed, a great leader knows that the reward was well worth the effort. Passing on knowledge can catch like wildfire, making it a very useful tool for leaders. You teach someone something that had a profound impact on you, and then he or she teaches another, and another, and so on and so forth. Then, all of a sudden, that same piece of knowledge ripples to hundreds or even thousands, instead of being contained in the mind of one.

In my opinion, teaching is a vastly underestimated leadership skill. A lot of emphasis is placed on coaching, and coaching is indeed very important, but coaching and teaching are two entirely different techniques used to pass on knowledge. Teaching provides the foundation of knowledge for coaching to build on. As children, we don't go to school to be coached, we go to school to be taught. Similarly, the new anglers on your boat first must be taught the fundamentals of leadership before they are expected to succeed. Without the fundamentals, they can not be properly coached and may never develop into the leaders they were meant to be. In your leadership practice remember to *Tie Their Knot* before trying to *Coach Their Cast*.

At the beginning of this chapter, I mentioned that the 3rd step of the *C.A.T.C.H. & Release* Model required a mental shift for leaders. This shift is one from a myopic mindset to that of a holistic mindset. Even though there is an "I" in leadership, it sits in the middle of the "ship." A ship sails not with a captain alone, but also a crew. As a leader, see the big picture of how your actions not only align with your own goals but also your crew's. Be proactive and intentional in how you choose to spend your time. Share knowledge, don't withhold it for self-serving reasons. Finally, find satisfaction in refraining from short-term distractions. Tie your passengers' knots every chance you get.

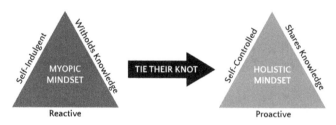

Having discussed the core elements that go into tying another's knot, it's important to note that the conversation does not end here. This is really just the beginning of developing others. Be careful not to fall into the trap of thinking, *I tied a new leader's knot, I checked that box, I'm done here.* If it were that easy, I think a lot more people would aspire to be great leaders; however, you already know that the work of a great leader is challenging and ongoing. Don't be the leader who ties another person's knot and walks away. Just as setting a dinner table doesn't ensure a great meal, tying a knot does not ensure a great *C.A.T.C.H. & Release.*

Coach Their Cast

Deliver Ongoing Feedback and Encouragement to Help Emerging Leaders Develop Their Own Skill Sets

"A good coach can change a game. A great coach can change a life."

-John Wooden

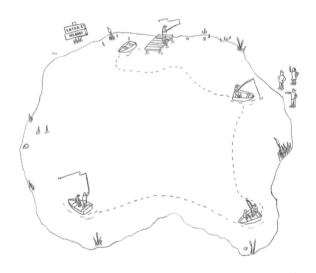

Leadership Constructs Discussed in *Coach Their Cast*
Deliberate Mindset • Providing Accurate Feedback
Instilling Ownership • Asking Thoughtful Questions
Discovering Learning Opportunities Unconditionally

"Wait a second..." I said in disbelief, *"I think I have a fish on."* The bite was subtle, I could have sworn it was just a light snag at first; however, after seeing the tension on my rod move up and down sporadically, I knew that a fish was on, but what kind of fish was it? It was the strangest thing, but as I began retrieving the fish in, I thought to myself this doesn't feel like a smallmouth bass. The fish wasn't very aggressive nor was it coming to the surface like smallies typically do. Doubts began to fill my head. *What if I hooked into a non-qualifying fish, a carp, catfish, or maybe even a muskie?* After all, Bob and I both caught a muskie during our practice round. Convincing myself that this fish was somehow flawed or may not even count toward the tournament, I began overthinking the situation and losing focus. Bob yelled, *"I'll grab the net! I can see it!"* As Bob extended the net over the boat to secure my catch, he confirmed it was indeed a keeper smallmouth bass. Trying my best to keep my rod tip up and tension on the line, I pulled the fish as close as I could to the side of the boat. Fully extended, Bob attempted to net the fish. The fish was just out of Bob's reach, when, suddenly, the tension on my line completely freed up. The fish spit the tube and zoomed back down to the rock pile. I couldn't believe it! The only bite I had all day, and it was a keeper that would have contributed to our team's total. Almost instantly, I started beating myself up, thinking that maybe I fished the retrieval wrong. I questioned myself. *Was I not ready for the hookset when the fish bit? Did I not maintain full tension on the line when I started thinking the fish wasn't a bass?* Agonizing for any excuse for why I lost the fish, I began examining the hook and knot. *Maybe it was the hook's fault, was it slightly bent or dulled?* I asked the boat driver and Bob if they had any new tube hooks, just to be safe, in case I got another chance. *Was it really the hook, or an error in my retrieval?* The truth is I will never know for sure, but in that situation, I desperately needed some kind of explanation. Trying to lift my spirits, both Bob and the boat driver encouraged me to continue with the dead stick method. They shared with me that sometimes smallies will clamp down on tubes without fully hooking themselves and then release their grip when they get close to the boat. I'm not sure their consolation

made me feel any better. What I wanted more than anything else in the world was to help the team out, which I was failing miserably at on that cold and dreary day.

––––––––––––

When fishing unknown waters, using unfamiliar techniques, or pursuing a new species of fish, a local fishing guide can greatly increase your chances for success. Guides spend years mastering their craft and possess tremendous amounts of knowledge and countless stories from past expeditions. They learn the ebbs and flows of the seasons, the nuances of the local fishing patterns, and the secret spots that seem to always produce fish. They take the guessing out of the sport for the prospective anglers they bring along. While success cannot always be guaranteed, guides can ensure a new experience and a well-thought-out plan of attack. In some ways, you may be inclined to think of fishing guides as coaches, but before arriving at that conclusion, it's important to understand the role coaching plays in leadership.

Although they share a lot of commonalities, leadership and coaching are not exactly synonymous with one another. It's true that both require a great deal of emotional intelligence, the ability to make timely decisions, and a passion to achieve collective results. Additionally, both require the ability to communicate effectively, persist through on-going obstacles, and adapt approaches when necessary. However, given the similarities, you still likely have two different mental schemas for what a great leader looks like and another one for what a great coach looks like. What are the unique qualities of a leader that differ from a coach? What specific behaviors are different? Can you think of a great leader who perhaps fits both molds?

For the purposes of this book, I view coaching as a significant part of leadership. Leaders who effectively coach others expand their impact and influence exponentially. Their legacy lives on through the number of lives they impact, skills they help develop, and goals they help others achieve. Coaching provides the supportive environment needed to overcome challenges, change thinking patterns, and promote personal growth. Great coaching experiences have the power to build trust and companionship like few other engagements on earth. With that being said, it's important to realize that coaching alone is not leadership. Being a great coach does not require you to be a great leader, but being a great leader definitely requires you to be a great coach.

Coach Their Cast, the 4th step in the *C.A.T.C.H. & Release* Model, highlights five leadership constructs aimed to increase your coaching effectiveness. Applying the knowledge outlined in this chapter will create giant waves in your ability to coach others. Take a moment to think of some of the greatest coaches you have had a chance to work with. When thinking about these coaches, ask yourself two questions: What methods did they use to help you achieve your goals? What kind of feedback did they deliver that still resonates with you today?

Keeping those same coaches in mind, ask yourself whether or not they were always your best friend. Did they do the work for you, providing you with the exact answer to every burning question you had, or did they help you arrive at the solution yourself? Metaphorically speaking, did they take you to the exact spot where the fish were, give you the perfect lure, and make sure you were successful in achieving your goals without any discomfort? My guess is that if they were great coaches, they didn't tell you the answers; they helped you discover them on your own. They didn't always provide the feedback you wanted to hear; they gave you the feedback you needed to hear. They didn't sugarcoat reality or make false promises about how easy the journey was going to be. They did, however, see something in you and believed in you. They held their tongues at times and harnessed the power of silence to make sure the messages you needed to hear didn't fall on deaf ears when the right time came. Even when you couldn't see learning opportunities during difficult times, your coaches did. Looking back, you realize they were there every step of the way, without judgment or criticism when you stumbled, but instead, encouraged you to get back on your feet. They guided you at the times that you could not guide yourself.

Great Coaches Don't Just Give You The Answers

To be a great coach requires you to possess a drive that expands beyond achieving an end result (e.g. a championship, new record, or personal fame). A coach's motivation must also be rooted in a humanistic desire to help others form sustainable habits and connections that promote long-term growth. Great coaches care about people. They value the process of development—just as much as, if not more than—any end result.

Jumping back to the topic of fishing guides that I referenced at the beginning of this chapter, I want you to consider some additional questions. Do you think fishing guides serve as examples of great coaches? To answer this question ask yourself what the primary goal and motivation of a guide is during the experience? Realizing that every guide's approach will be slightly different (and this is not a knock on fishing guides) I think it's safe to say that a guide's primary objective is to put as many fish into the boat as quickly and efficiently as possible. Given the dynamic of the relationship, they are less likely to spend time coaching (i.e. asking thoughtful questions, instilling ownership, discovering learning opportunities, etc.) and more likely providing you with answers. The long-term development of their clients is probably a secondary goal compared to creating a memorable experience and landing a five-star review on their Yelp account. Think about it, the majority of their time is spent preparing equipment, driving the boat, and handling the catches that come on-board—not coaching to all of the individual skill sets of their passengers. Last but not least, consider their communication style, which tends to be more directive (e.g. *"Cast right there!"*) than it is inquisitive (e.g. *"Where do you think a good place to cast is?"*). This subtle, yet meaningful distinction is an important one as you consider the role coaching plays in leadership.

Developing the skills needed to be a great coach will allow you to impact others in unimaginable ways, but where does one start? A fishing rod, of course. The keys to effective coaching can be found attached to nearly every fishing rod. The narrowing circles found at the base of the rod play such a critical role in the fishing experience.

These often-overlooked attachments serve to guide your line during a cast, provide continuous feedback to help you understand the environment beneath the water, and serve as a safety mechanism in the lure-retrieval process. When you set your hook, these guides help you distinguish the difference between a fish and a snag. Without the guides, the strength of the rod would never absorb the tension from your line. Your line would have no connection to the rod, leaving you unable to leverage your full potential in setting hooks and reeling in the fish you seek to catch. Throughout the process, these fishing guides help you improve as an angler through the feedback they provide, allowing you to fine-tune your casting and hook-setting skills over time. Fishing without these guides greatly inhibits an angler's success, and leading others without coaching them is essentially asking them to fish with a guideless rod. Left absent of the proper mechanisms and ongoing support to grow, the anglers on your boat will fail to realize their full potential.

The Fishing Guides of Coaching

Great leaders understand that no two people are exactly the same. They realize that the best way to help others is not to force them into a specific mold of leadership, but rather to help them form a unique leadership mold for themselves. In Chapter One, *Cast Your Line*, I outlined different casting techniques of leadership. Every leader comes to the lake with different fishing equipment and varying levels of mastery relating to specific casting techniques. Great coaches understand that their job is not to coerce others to cast the exact same way they do, but rather use their knowledge and experience to help others master their own casts.

THE BASICS OF COACHING

Before outlining each of *The Five Guides of Coaching*, it's important for all leaders to revisit some of the basics:

First, coaching conversations should always be tied to the goals of the coachee. Goals are important because they serve as the anchor for developmental activities and feedback while also allowing for progress to be tracked throughout the process. It's important the goals are *S.M.A.R.T.* (specific, measurable, attainable, relevant, time-bound) and fully owned by the coachee.

Second, it's important to clarify if the coaching being provided is part of a formal coaching engagement (e.g. 6-month coaching plan) or more informal in nature (e.g. unstructured without a definitive timeline). Regardless of the agreed-upon structure, keep in mind that the best coaches do not have lifelong coachees. Instead, great coaches intentionally provide guidance and support for a specific stretch in their coachee's journey. Regardless of the coaching framework (formal or informal), always cherish and never take for granted the momentary role you get to play in your coachee's development.

Third, let your coachees know upfront what type of coach you are by outlining your own strengths and development areas as well as the ways you plan to make yourself available to coach them. Perhaps you choose to block off weekly office hours dedicated to coaching, or you communicate to your team that you prefer providing real-time coaching by pulling them aside, closely after an event they were engaged in. Whatever arrangements you agree upon, make sure to let others know that coaching is a skill you value as a leader. Inform them that you are not only willing to coach, but that you will prioritize it to aid their development. The next generation of leaders are hungry for coaching, let them know you are ready to deliver it.

Fourth, note that your communication style will need to adapt to your audience. Since no two people are the same, no two coaching messages will ever be received exactly the same way. What will resonate with some coachees may not resonate with others. This is why it is so important, as a leader, to understand the unique motivations, skill sets, and communication styles of the people you coach upfront. Keep in mind that there is no boilerplate or one-size-fits-all coaching style. To be great, you must be willing to continuously learn and adapt your approach as you develop as a leader.

There Is No One-Size-Fits-All Coaching Style

Finally, it is important to understand the profound impact you can have as a coach. People who seek your coaching are willing to show you their vulnerabilities. Be conscious of your actions; your coaching behavior has the power to change lives. Make sure your intentions are pure and come from a place of benevolence.

THE FIVE GUIDES OF COACHING

What sets good coaches apart from great ones? The answer is practice and a desire to keep getting better. Once a coach becomes comfortable with the basics, they must strive to expand their coaching skills through the application of more advanced coaching concepts. *The Five Guides of Coaching* were designed to help you do just that—up your coaching game—from JV to Varsity. Reaching beyond the basics, *The Five Guides of Coaching* require much more mental and physical practice to master. Improving on these five constructs will not only make you a better coach but will also change the way you view effective coaching from now on.

Coaching Guide #1: Deliberate Mindset
The ability to refrain from impulsive thoughts and actions.

As I've mentioned, great coaches understand that every coachee is unique; therefore, labels or quick judgments only cloud a coach's ability to see a situation for what it really is. While it's important to leverage past learnings as a coach, avoid jumping to conclusions too soon. There are no cookie-cutter approaches to effective coaching. You must view each coaching engagement as a new opportunity to guide a future leader on their *own* journey. Understanding and applying a deliberate mindset will reduce the number of initial assumptions you make blinding your ability to see your coachee's unique perspectives. Being deliberate in your thoughts and actions is mutually beneficial because it allows for unique conversations and learning to unfold in a more meaningful way helping both the coach and coachee hone their skills over time. In life, people want to believe that their challenges are unique; therefore, they want to be developed and coached in a way that also feels unique—this requires being deliberate.

Let's face it, coaching is difficult work and it will test you. Some days your coachee will cooperate like an angel, and other days, not so much. Remember, the emotional roller coaster is all part of the ride. Regardless of the ups and downs, you must stay above it mentally. It's essential that you fight the urge to channel your inner Bobby Knight (notoriously hot-blooded, yet legendary Indiana Hoosier Basketball Coach) and throw a chair across the court (he actually did that) when things don't go as planned. No matter how bleak a situation seems in the moment, or how many times your coachee fails, you must fight your impulse to speak or act in a way that will hinder his or her's future development. Even if the answer or advice you are trying to convey is blatantly obvious, the context, emotions, and delivery of the message must be deliberate. Regardless of how irritated or downright pissed off you may be in the moment; you must demonstrate the wisdom to separate impulsive emotion from the greater objective of strategic growth.

Your job as a coach is not to *fix* people. I'll repeat that, your job is *not to fix* people! Instead, your aim should be to help people fix themselves, and that takes time. Do not confuse coaching with the practice of providing unsolicited advice to help solve all the things that are *"wrong"* with your coachee. If you go around trying to fix people with your so-called *"advice,"* you'll find your messages falling on deaf ears, not supporting behavioral change, and potentially causing more harm than good. Instead, focus your deliberate attention on ways you can empower others to solve their own problems. Seek to build their confidence, increase their awareness, and challenge them to challenge themselves. The key to your effectiveness will largely depend on both the timing and intentionality of your messaging. Experienced coaches refrain from impulsively calling out flaws in the moment; instead, they deliberately promote the right learning opportunities in the right place at the right time which requires a high level of emotional intelligence.

As A Coach, Your Job Is Not To Fix People

To put all of this in context, take some time to think about someone you know well—a significant other, a friend, or even a coworker who does something that drives you absolutely crazy. Maybe it's the way they chew their gum, slurp fluid through a straw, or always show up late for meetings. Over time it's easy to let an annoying behavior or pattern of annoying behaviors create a label of that person. Perhaps you start thinking of them as *'neat freaks'* or, on the opposite end of the spectrum, *'slobs'*? You wish they would just recognize and change some of their mannerisms, which would make them far better off. All humans have these thoughts from time to time. There are certain things that will simply drive you crazy; however, you must learn how to pick and choose your battles. This is especially true as a coach. Demonstrating an inability to hold your tongue while simultaneously possessing a constant need to *"fix"* all the habits of your coachees will end poorly for you. Sooner or later, your coachees will become overwhelmed with all your advice and even get defensive. Over time, they will start using selective hearing, allowing some of the advice you give to go in one ear and out the other. If you're not deliberate, this may eventually cause you to snap, saying something irrational or emotional in the heat of the moment when perceived development isn't occurring quickly enough. How effective is picking every single battle when trying to create lasting change in others? You already know the answer—not very effective at all. This is because behavioral change is most effective and sustainable when the change is something your coachees are motivated to do for their own intrinsic reasons, not just to avoid your constant badgering. A more effective method is to deliberately articulate the benefits that changing the behavior will have for your coachees. Sprinkle in a few of your own experiences and stories that highlight positive outcomes resulting from changing your own behavior.

Remember, the key to sparking change in another is having your coachees connect the dots for themselves. The goal is to create a desire from within your coachees to make the change. Help them come up with the idea to change, instead of trying to tell them what they "*should do.*" People tend to have negative reactions when nagged, and, in some cases, will do the opposite. Great coaches understand this, that's why they tend to be less authoritarian in their communication methods. Instead, they opt to use a form of Socratic Method (asking thoughtful questions) to promote sustainable change. Possessing a deliberate mindset and knowing how and when to pick your battles will go a long way in your ability to effectively coach others.

Coaching Guide #2: Providing Accurate Feedback

The ability to constructively communicate strengths and development areas in others using behavioral examples.

Feedback is the food that fuels development. It nourishes self-awareness and provides guidance to growth. It can act as either the catalyst or paralyzer of potential, depending on how it is prepared and served. As the coach, you play the role of the chef. One of your core responsibilities is to prepare and dish up balanced portions of feedback to help your coachees achieve their goals. What's on the menu may not always be what your coachees want to eat, but they can rest assured knowing the dishes are prepared with 100% organic, behavioral-based ingredients.

What is behavioral-based feedback and why is it so important to coaching? Behavioral-based feedback is the most objective and pragmatic form of feedback. It is anchored in the specific actions of an individual. Put simply, behavioral-based feedback is tied directly to the verbal and nonverbal behaviors an individual displays. Grounding feedback in behaviors reduces subjectivity and bias which you know from Chapter 2, *Attract Diverse Anglers,* can be detrimental to great leadership. Using behaviors, such as specific quotes and actions, to discuss feedback makes the job easier for both the person delivering the message as well as the receiver. To help you remember this idea, think of your role as a leader like a camera when collecting feedback. Playing the tape back, you can see the actual behavior and hear the audio of what was said. What's not pre-programmed on the device is speculation and subjective interpretation. This approach removes conjecture from the equation, which only clouds feedback at the end of the day. Contrary to what some people may think, the receiver is actually more likely to openly accept feedback in a behavior-based form. They view it as more fair, objective, and personal to their own development. Having had the privilege of delivering feedback to hundreds of leaders during assessment centers early on in my career, I can wholeheartedly say that no matter how positive or negative the feedback was, if it was tied to behavior and coming from a good place, leaders were receptive.

Keen observation is key to documenting behavioral-based feedback. It takes practice and the cognitive ability to quickly decipher which behaviors are most relevant to a coachee's development. As a coach, you must find the sweet spot of delivering just the right amount of feedback to nurture growth. Too much feedback can flood people with confusion or feelings of being overwhelmed as they try to process all the data points. On the flip side, inadequate amounts of feedback can stunt growth and engagement, leaving blind spots unexposed. The aim as a coach should be to provide the highest quality feedback, in digestible portions, empowering coachees to commit to action.

Determining what behaviors are most important to document should stem from the previously discussed goals of the coachee. Your job is not to follow your coachees around with a clipboard and document every single behavior they display in a given day, but rather to hone in on the ones that will make the greatest difference in their development. For instance, if you were coaching an individual who has set a developmental goal to become a more effective presenter, you would want to distinguish the behaviors that are most meaningful to presenting. Instead of observing and providing feedback on how your coachee interacts with coworkers in the breakroom or at a team lunch, it would better serve you to prioritize your observation efforts on an upcoming sales pitch your coachee is delivering to a board of directors. During that sales pitch, your attention should be dialed in and ready to document behaviors related to the tone of the opening statement: the eye contact of your coachee, his or her ability to answer impromptu questions with poise and confidence, etc. Documenting an unexpected sneeze or a technological issue that was no fault of your coachee will inhibit your ability to capture the most meaningful bits of feedback your coachee needs to develop in his or her pre-identified skill gap.

Equally as important to capturing meaningful behaviors is to understand the situation, your coachee's intention, and the ultimate impact of the behavior. For instance, his or her intention may have been to open the presentation to the board with a charismatic welcome; however, you may have observed a fidgety and pacing presenter who forgot to make introductions and jumped right into the presentation prematurely. The impact of the behavior resulted in a senior board member interrupting the presentation one minute in to ask who the presenter was and what the purpose of the presentation was.

Capturing behavioral-based feedback is an important skill to learn, but the delivery of feedback is where the greater challenge lies for many coaches. Documenting meaningful feedback without delivering it to your coachees out of fear of how it will come across can be detrimental to their development. While it's sometimes difficult to tell people that their actions were not par for the course, your responsibility as a coach is to tell your coachees what you've observed regardless of how good or bad it was. If you can't muster the courage to deliver the message, how can you honestly expect them to grow? This point goes for both positive and negative feedback. Not giving people positive feedback because you expect good performance from them can lead to unnecessary worry and doubt in the minds of your coachees. Acknowledging a good job, even when you expect a good job, can do wonders to boost self-esteem in a coachee. Don't forget, as a coach, that a little bit of praise can go a long way. Also, keep in mind that the term 'feedback' can immediately make some people think they did something wrong. Changing this perception is something you can do by delivering balanced portions of positive and negative feedback. Over time, your coachees will start to crave the feedback you put on the menu, as long as you continue to master your culinary gift.

Here are some pointers to keep in mind as you develop your ability to provide meaningful feedback:

1. Find time to deliver the feedback close to the time when the behaviors were captured (while the situation is still fresh in both of your minds).

2. Make sure the receiver is open to getting your feedback prior to delivering it. Simply ask them if they would like to hear what you observed.

3. Before delivering the feedback, ask the receiver to self-reflect on how they thought a specific situation/experience went. Then, listen closely to what they say. You may be surprised by how self-aware they are of their strengths and weaknesses. Make sure to ask them about their intention going into the situation and the ultimate impact of their actions.

4. When delivering your message, avoid the commonly used '*feedback sandwich*' (positive comment, negative comment,

positive comment) which can confuse people from easily deciphering the key messages they need to hear. Instead, focus on building authentic relationships where all forms of behavioral-based feedback are welcomed from a place of trust and continuous improvement.

5. Deliver your feedback with courage—do not sugarcoat or downplay it. This may be the only time in their life that they hear it. It is far better to bear a few moments of discomfort than to go a lifetime wishing you would have said something.

6. Provide the receiver with time to process and ask questions about the feedback you delivered. Sometimes feedback can catch people off guard, and they may need time to process it.

7. Always leave the receiver feeling empowered to leverage their feedback regardless of how positive or constructive it was. The whole purpose of feedback is to provide a tangible path forward, not to crush a person's spirits or stroke their ego.

Over time, your ability to capture and deliver behavioral-based feedback will improve. You will begin to quickly pick up on the most meaningful behaviors and the impacts those behaviors have on a situation. You will not shy away from delivering difficult feedback; instead, you will deliver it in a way that empowers others to make changes. Remember that feedback is a two-way street—create an environment that encourages others to give you feedback, too. Their feedback will not only help you in the future but also provide your coachees an opportunity to practice the same skill you just demonstrated. Lastly, never underestimate the important role that listening plays in the feedback process. Listen to understand your coachees, not just to respond. Your coachees will be able to tell the difference, and more importantly, they will likely mirror the same listening behavior as you. So be present and really listen. If you follow these steps I promise that you will create a lasting appetite for feedback in others.

Coaching Guide #3: Instilling Ownership

Building accountability in others to follow through on their commitments.

Success in any area of life largely depends on the ability to follow through. Without it, even the best-laid plans evaporate when initial excitement fades. For most people, long-term commitments can be scary; they require sacrifices, changes in behavior, and accepting the possibility of failure. Great leaders understand that there are both risks and rewards associated with being held accountable, but unlike those who let failure lead to paralysis, great leaders own their outcomes for better or worse.

As a coach, you play a vital role in developing others, and one of the best ways to set your coachees up for long-term success is to instill a sense of ownership in them. Help them learn how to own both the successes and failures of their experiences in a healthy and productive way. Remember that their journeys are just that—*their own*. Your job is to guide them on their journeys, not carry them across the finish line. Focus your efforts on strengthening their abilities, removing mental roadblocks, and inspiring them to stretch themselves in new ways. Instead of carrying the weight for them, you must find ways to keep them feeling light, energized, and confident as they take each new step forward.

The ability to instill ownership begins when you help your coachees realize what they are, and are not in control of. Life isn't always fair, and, as a coach, it is important to acknowledge that certain aspects of your coachees' reality were predetermined outside of their control (e.g. their family dynamic, ethnicity, genetic health conditions, etc.). While it's OK to acknowledge these facts of life, spending too much time ruminating on what is not in their control will inhibit your ability to instill ownership in them. Rather, your interactions should focus more on the desired outcomes, behavioral changes, and subsequent actions they can take now resulting in future success. Help them shift their mindset so they are able to feel more confident in their ability to positively influence the outcomes in their lives. No matter the challenge, or unexpected circumstance, your coachees have the ability to own their responses, help them see that by remembering the equation $E + R = O$ (Events + Responses = Outcome) (Canfield, 2019). While certain events both inside and outside of their control will transpire, coachees will always be able to influence their success (outcome) by owning their response.

Understanding your coachee's motivation and vision will also be paramount to instilling ownership in them. Both elements help drive accountability and persistence when met with resistance. When coachees are unable to clearly articulate their motivation and goals, it becomes nearly impossible for a coach to help instill ownership in them. Phrases like, *"I'm not sure what I really want"* or *"The goal I set was stupid, I never thought I could achieve it anyway"* drive coaches crazy. Without clear direction, measurable outcomes, and a strong *"why"*, ownership slips through the cracks one excuse at a time.

Bring Goals To Life Through Visualization

To help bring goals to life in your coachees, ask them to define (and articulate) what future success looks like. Ask them what their internal motivation is propelling them to achieve what it is they have yet to achieve. Ask them to describe in extreme detail what it feels like to achieve their goal before they actually accomplish it. Use specific questions, such as: *"What emotions are you experiencing? What are you wearing as you are recognized for your accomplishments? Who is cheering you on? What does it smell like? What song is playing in the background?"* Questions like these, as random as they might sound, help bring a vision to life and instill a greater sense of ownership in making their dreams a reality. This exercise not only benefits them but also you, the coach, by providing you the context that you need to encourage them on the days they begin to doubt themselves.

The last step required for a coach seeking to instill ownership is to walk away when the time is right. This will vary from coachee to coachee depending on the progress made, but remember the ultimate long-term goal for your coachees is to own their accountability independently. Formal coaches and trainers, no matter how great they are, should not be hired indefinitely; it's not sustainable nor is it a leading practice for long-term development. When the time is right you must allow your coachees to fly on their own. It's OK if they feel an initial void in your absence, if you did your job well they should be equipped with the visualization and motivational tools to propel them forward.

Building on what was discussed earlier in the *C.A.T.C.H. & Release* Model, keep in mind your coachees are responsible for casting their own lines as they develop into leaders. It won't be long before they are captaining their own boats. Before they depart on that journey, it's your job to help them own their realities. Instill ownership in them and help them visualize their unique "*why.*" Remind them that failure is part of the journey and that they will never achieve any of the goals they don't to set for themselves. Give them the nudge they need and serve as the role model for them to someday coach others. Lastly, help them embrace their own uniqueness and remind them that no one can lead them better than they can lead themselves. By doing so, you will have expanded your impact and legacy exponentially.

Coaching Guide #4: Asking Thoughtful Questions
The ability to ask open-ended questions in a way that allows others to draw meaningful conclusions.

There is no such thing as a dumb question… or is there? You have probably heard the '*dumb question*' saying used a thousand times in a classroom or training setting. The intention is to encourage participation from the audience (or students) regardless of their comprehension level. To a curious mind, there are no dumb questions. Questions and their appropriate answers are the building blocks of learning, and curious minds should continue to ask questions to make new connections. To that end, does the same principle hold true for enlightened minds? Does the phrase, *"there are no dumb questions,"* apply to the teacher the same way it does their students? As a coach, you are viewed as the teacher more so than the student; therefore, your questions should be more selective and deliberate by nature. I fully recognize that coaching and teaching are not the same things and that many coaches could argue they learn as much from their coaching interactions as their coachees do, but, at the end of the day, you are sought after because you possess something your counterpart doesn't: knowledge and an ability to promote behavioral change. The questions you use should nourish new growth and stretch your coachees to think outside of the box. Your questions cannot be too easy, leading your coachees to feel patronized, but they can't be too difficult either, leading to self-doubt. As tempting as it may be to avoid using questions altogether and just tell your coachees what you think they should do, it will be far less effective than your coachees drawing their own conclusions based on the questions you ask. Great coaches have a knack for asking the right questions at the right time to promote new learning. To be a better coach, and ultimately a better leader, it's time to up your question game.

Back in grad school, I had a classmate who wholeheartedly swore that people will always be tempted to do the opposite of what they're told to do. It sounds sinister, but she passionately believed it and still does to this day. This idea leads me to ask you if you have ever experienced a friend, child, or significant other doing the opposite of what you asked them out of spite or pure curiosity about the consequence? *Reverse psychology* is the popular term you have likely heard used to describe this idea. The phenomenon ties to coaching and, more specifically, asking thoughtful questions for two reasons.

First, simply telling coachees to do something may be less effective than you think. While a lot of factors are involved with your coachees' decisions to act on your instructions (e.g. the regard in which they hold you, the clarity of your message, and how it resonates to their own viewpoint), it may actually prompt thoughts or actions in the opposite direction. The reality is that many people do not like to follow instructions if it feels like something they *have to* do. Of course, personality and cultural differences make it hard to generalize this phenomenon across an entire population—but consider your audience. If you are coaching current or aspiring leaders, they likely prefer to challenge conventional wisdom and act as mavericks from time to time. Remember this when you are tempted to provide them with precise instructions on what to do. Could a question serve as a better alternative to drive behavior?

Second, never use reverse psychology to try to influence your coachees to do the opposite of what you would really like for them to do. Even if you consider yourself a Jedi Master who can use mind tricks to influence others, you will find yourself in a lot of trouble if you go around telling your coachees to do the opposite of what you really want them to do in hopes that they will act in a way that counters your instructions. Instead, use more questions than statements to guide your coachees. Empower them to draw their own conclusions based on what is best for their growth. This will ultimately promote stronger learning connections and greater commitment to action because the solutions will be self-generated.

Now that I have primed your brain with one Star Wars reference, I can't help but channel my inner Yoda for the next. *"So, a leader you seek to be hmm!? Learn how to ask thoughtful questions you ask, teach you I must!"* Apologizes to any non-Star Wars fans, but Yoda truly is the master of asking thoughtful questions. So, let's dive in. First things first, you have to learn how to really listen. The best way to ask thoughtful questions, ones that really challenge assumptions at their core and open new ways of thinking, is to fully understand where your coachees are coming from. Make sure to listen in detail to how they describe their current goals, challenges, and motivations guiding them to lead. Find out what's worked well for them in the past and what hasn't. Document and remember the specifics—the more context you can gather, the better your questions will hit home. If you don't feel like writing your notes down, use a voice recorder to summarize your own thoughts following important conversations. Second, learn how to harness the power of silence. Silence is the loudest and most uncomfortable sound a person will hear when asked deeply reflective questions. For many people, regardless of the social setting, silence is something that is avoided like the great plague. You will know this when your coachee begins using filler statements like *"um"* or begins backpedaling, trying to dodge the question with unrelated banter. Silence, though, should not be shied away from as a coach. It can not only prompt a meaningful response, but it can also allow time for an individual to process and arrive at new learnings. The uncomfortable feeling silence creates can serve as a powerful tool if leveraged correctly. Unlike words, the volume of silence can't be turned down.

Silence Is The Loudest Sound

To use a coaching metaphor related to sports, think of all the times you've seen a coach berate players on the sidelines immediately after missing opportunities on the field. Prior to the public shaming, there is a good chance the players have already realized the mistakes they recently made. Yelling in a fit of rage only adds animosity and anxiety to the situation. Even worse, it may diminish confidence in the players' ability to improve the situation moving forward. Instead of acting impulsively, the coach should take notes, allow time for emotions to subside, and then ask the thoughtful questions the players need to learn from their mistakes. Those precious moments of silence after a mishap can be much more effective at fostering development than screaming in a player's face.

Lastly, eliminate expectations of the type of responses you want to hear related to the thoughtful questions you ask. If the questions you ask are truly thought-provoking, they shouldn't evoke cookie-cutter responses. Regardless of how the coachees respond, their answers will be telling. Remove your expectations and simply listen. Throughout this process, remember that your coachees are unique, their answers may be different than your own, but that's what makes them special. Avoid being overly judgmental as they attempt to answer your questions. Instead, seek to learn more about why they answered it the way they did, and how you can use that information to better tailor your coaching.

To summarize, here are some helpful tips that can improve your ability to ask thoughtful questions and ultimately become a more effective coach:

1. Understand the context, concerns, and motivation your coachees have toward their goals.
2. Listen and identify current gaps in their understanding.
3. Ask a series of open-ended questions to help them connect the dots.
4. Harness the power of silence when waiting for a response.
5. Give them credit for drawing their own conclusions and path forward; this will help instill ownership.
6. Remove any expectation for the way your coachee should be answering your question.

Coaching Guide #5: Discovering Learning Opportunities Unconditionally

The ability to find meaningful lessons regardless of the situation.

Have you ever noticed that the best coaches always seem to have something profound to say? They uplift spirits during times of great difficulty, as well as ground others during times of great fortune. The best coaches understand that learning opportunities are the seeds to growth. They understand that every experience, no matter how big or small, has a lesson that can be harvested. This ability to unconditionally find silver linings in almost every situation is a tremendous attribute of a great leader. And—surprise, surprise—this coaching skill also requires a significant amount of emotional intelligence. To be successful, one must be able to empathize and communicate opportunities in a way that resonates with the sentiment of a coachee. This requires a great deal of tact. As a coach, you must be fully aware of your coachees' environment, so that you don't kick them when they are down, nor inflate their egos when they are up. Discovering learning opportunities in both good and bad situations will greatly bolster your ability to coach.

On the water, anglers, just like leaders, benefit greatly when tuning into the daily lessons life throws at them. Every day, rain or shine, a unique opportunity presents itself to learn something new. Whether it's something related to the fishing environment, an angler's strengths and development areas, or how to deal with the adversity mother nature unexpectedly brews up— many lessons surface just waiting to be caught. Even on the days when an angler gets skunked (not catching a single fish), invaluable knowledge, however painful it may be in the moment, can still be gained. Through reflection on the techniques and lures that did not produce results during a given day, an angler gains insight on how to adapt fishing techniques to produce better results on the next outing. On opposite days (where it seems like fish are just jumping into the boat), an angler can take note of the conditions, the lure, and the techniques producing results, in order to replicate the same success at a later date. The beauty of fishing is that the patterns and seasons are always changing, just like the experiences in your life; therefore, it's imperative to learn the lesson any given moment is teaching you to better prepare yourself for the future.

Effectively coaching others requires a similar mindset. You need to be adaptive and always look for the next great lesson your coachees need on their developmental journey. The art of discovering and sharing new learning opportunities with your coachees requires balance. Focus on enhancing the learning—regardless of the outcome—with insight and perspective. Your tone should be similar to, yet just slightly different from, the emotion your coachees are experiencing. You do not want to mirror exactly what it is they are feeling, but you want to meet them where they are emotionally and offer a slightly new perspective on the situation. For instance, if your coachees are beating themselves up over a mistake they made, acknowledge the struggle, but offer a slightly more optimistic outlook. Strike a balance, and do not be too over the top. You likely have experienced a time when you were feeling down and someone said something that was a bit out of tune with the situation? Perhaps something like *"Turn that frown upside down!"* or *"Cheer up buttercup!"* when the person didn't even make an attempt to understand the situation? Even if the intention was to help you, the messaging comes across as insensitive and out of touch. Even worse, it doesn't provide any constructive learning. Trying to coach others this way can lead to more frustration and resentment later on. A more effective approach is to show empathy and acknowledge the situation for what it is—a challenge—but also an opportunity to grow. Once a person feels like they have been understood, they will be much more likely to consider alternative perspectives and be open to changing their thoughts and actions. Even when mistakes are made by your coachees, use the mistakes as opportunities to build from. If your coachees are willing to accept responsibility and apply the lessons they learned from the mistake in the future, they will be much better off for it.

Similarly, when coachees experience great success, coaches shouldn't rain on their parade or feel the need to play devil's advocate. Instead, celebrate with them and help them solidify the lessons they learned by having them reflect on some of the hardships they had to overcome leading up to their success. Meet your coachees wherever they are at emotionally and offer a slightly new angle to enhance their learning. If it helps, visualize your coachees' emotions as a temperature reading on a thermometer. The learning opportunities you provide in a situation should be within a few degrees of the emotional temperature of your coachees. Anything drastically hot or cold will not resonate. Strive to always add value to the situation, instead of just reinforcing the current emotions of your coachees. Simply telling them how hot or cold they look (i.e. happy or sad) based on their emotional thermometer will provide little value and may inhibit the ability for them to take something meaningful away from the situation. Instead, check in to see where they are emotionally in the moment and communicate the learning that will be of the greatest benefit to them. As a coach, set yourself up for success by discovering learning opportunities regardless of the situation. If you do so, you will always be prepared to deliver a meaningful locker room speech—whether your team just got beat at the buzzer or won the state title.

Effectively demonstrating *The Five Guides of Coaching* requires mental discipline. There is a fundamental difference between mastering your own cast and helping others master theirs. It takes time, patience, and an intrinsic desire to pass on learning. Your legacy as a leader will not be solidified by hoarding the knowledge that you have acquired. It will be solidified based on your ability to use that knowledge to develop other leaders who can innovate, adapt, and carry the leadership torch you lit to impact the world in a positive way. This doesn't mean there won't be snags along the way. Your job is to help others get over their fear of snagging and start catching what matters most—leadership.

S.N.A.G. to F.I.S.H.

Every angler—just like every leader—will undoubtedly snag their line from time to time. Snags come in all shapes and sizes. You make a bad cast, throw the wrong lure, your equipment fails, etc. all ending with the same result—you get hung up. Mistakes come with the territory. By casting yourself out there as a leader, you will inevitably catch situations or failures you did not intend to catch. The process of snagging requires you to embrace your vulnerabilities as a means to growth.

As a coach, help your coachees understand that snags are part of the learning process and that a healthy relationship needs to be established with them. Help them understand that losing their cool every time unexpected adversity comes along will only lead to more hardships. Since many of those you coach will be high achievers, embracing snags, or failure in general, may not be an easy concept for them to grasp. Your job is to help them understand that snagging, not catching, is what hooking into leadership is all about.

A few summers ago, I found myself dealing with a snag in my own career. I had spent a year and a half working toward the goal of being promoted at a reputable consulting firm. I had spent countless hours volunteering for additional projects, building my network in the organization, and honing my consulting skills in the talent management space. In the end, all the experience I gained was far worth the effort, but that still didn't lessen the blow when I was told that I was not being promoted to manager. I felt embarrassed, ashamed, and started to question my own self-worth. To add insult to injury, a number of my colleagues knew I was up for the promotion, which made it all the worse when I realized they would find out I wasn't going to make the cut that year. I experienced a whole host of emotions that week at work; but, in the middle of it all, I remembered something important, something referenced earlier in this chapter. *You can't always control the outcome of an event, but you can always control how you react to it.* It was disappointing—it really was—but I allowed myself the time to feel all the emotions involved with getting hung up on that snag early on in my career.

I am a firm believer that people need time to process thoughts and feelings when dealing with adversity. The amount of time can vary from person to person, but it is very important to allow oneself to truly feel the emotions. If you don't, you may feel resentment later on and fail to discover key learning opportunities from the situation. On the flip side, there is a danger in allowing yourself to ruminate or victimize yourself too long over your hardships. Instead, strive for a balance, allow yourself to feel your emotions at first, and then collect yourself and come up with an intentional plan to improve your outlook on the situation. Some of the greatest life lessons come from the adversities we experience. Always be open to the lessons that present themselves, even if you can't see them immediately.

In my case, it came down to me needing to make a new decision about my future. What did I really want, and how could I use the disappointment as a learning opportunity in my own development? About two weeks after receiving the news, I came to peace with the decision. It still hurt, but I needed to find a way to turn it into something productive, not destructive. Reflecting back now, not being promoted was one of the best things that could have happened to me at that time. It allowed me to reconsider several competing priorities in my life and put me on a new path to follow my true calling. To do so, I intentionally changed my perspective on the situation. I started opening up about my hardship, not concealing it, in the hopes that it could help others cope with their own challenges. I didn't let my vulnerability eat at me, I decided to use it for good. I realized that I needed to own not getting promoted, feel the disappointment, and come up with a plan to use the setback as a way to accomplish something I never thought possible. Our flaws and hardships are what make us human; they can serve us in ways that lead to tremendous growth when we decide to let them.

Seeing leaders from all backgrounds deal with adversity, I have come to realize that there is a mindset associated with turning failures into positive learning experiences. It starts with understanding your mind and limiting the damage negative thoughts can have from unexpected hardships. The next time you experience a failure in your life, apply these four steps of the *S.N.A.G.*

Survey the Situation

When facing a difficult setback, take a second to survey where you are physically, mentally, and emotionally. Take a deep breath and try to see the big picture. The initial shock or disappointment can sometimes get the best of you and make you lose focus of the long game. Keep in mind that others are watching how you choose to respond to the situation. When emotions run high, take a deep breath and remember that a lure can easily be replaced, but a reputation cannot.

Neutralize the Negativity

Negative thoughts lead to negative behaviors. The vicious cycle can be broken—it starts with acceptance and awareness. Accept the fact that negativity will surface periodically, and build greater awareness to the triggers that cause it. Although seeds of negativity may already be planted in your mind, they do not need to grow. Becoming more aware of your thoughts and the language you use when dealing with adversity is the first step in stunting the growth of negativity. Failures are only damaging when you allow negativity to snowball. The moment you stop blaming outside forces and accept your failure as an opportunity to grow is the moment you begin to neutralize negativity. Recognizing your negativity and minimizing its impact provides you new space to change the story.

Adapt your perspective

As the author of your own story, you get to choose the narrative to which others listen. The pages that fill up your book will be determined by how you respond to the challenges in your life. As your story unfolds, remember that everyone in life deals with adversity, but not everyone takes ownership of their story. Do not take a backseat and let life write the book for you. Instead, proactively decide to pick up your pen and write the perspective you want to create.

"If you aren't snagging, you aren't catching" is a common saying among anglers. When you cast into areas with a lot of structure and obstacles, you will occasionally get hung up, but that's where the fish reside. Changing your perspective on failure will help you navigate hardships in a new light. Leaders need to fail in order to learn and continuously improve—it's all part of the story. Fail fast and fail smart, but keep on failing. Remember that if you aren't snagging, you aren't leading.

Gain new insights

Regardless of the type of failure or let down you may have just experienced, find comfort in knowing that there is still a lesson for you to learn. Something greater than the moment, something worth persevering through. Snags will continue to irritate you until you learn what they are trying to tell you. The hidden lessons beneath the water allow you to see something you hadn't before. Snags force you to slow down and really understand the environment in which you are trying to succeed.

Learn how to self-reflect in a way that drives deep-rooted learning when life throws you hardships. Use snags as ways to challenge your old thinking patterns and limiting beliefs about yourself. This may require you to find a place that allows you to solely focus on the situation, behavior, and impact of whatever issue you are trying to remedy. Once you are there, and initial emotions have subsided, try to learn something new that you otherwise wouldn't have learned if the snag hadn't happened. Write down what the failure is and what opportunities it provides for your growth. Write down what exactly it is you learned and how you plan to apply the new insight into your day-to-day activities. It may sound basic, but if you aren't intentional in collecting your thoughts, you may miss all the new insights presented to you. At times, it may even feel like you are snagging the same log you have been hung up on for years, but know there is still something new to be learned there. I encourage you to spend time discovering all the new knowledge that is being presented to you. The answers are out there and they will help you develop into a better leader in the future. Over time, you will learn to snag with grace. You will not fear failure, but rather crave the new insights it provides. Stay calm and learn from all the amazing lessons life gives you through your snags. Keep in mind that the best snags in life come when you finally decide to *F.I.S.H.*

FIND YOUR PASSION

Understanding your passion in life will motivate you to achieve great things. It will serve as a guiding force that centers you through thick and thin. It will also inspire others to fulfill their own dreams. Undoubtedly your passion(s) will change over the course of your leadership career and that's okay. New experiences will generate new passions and a deeper desire to become the greatest version of yourself. Likely, you know deep down what you are being called to do right now, but resist it out of fear of failure or judgment from others. To be an effective leader, you must not only know what your passion is but also act on it. If not, regret or remorse may inhibit your ability to realize your potential. Do the reflective work, ask yourself the tough questions, and align your day-to-day activities in a way that feeds your inner calling.

INTERNALIZE THE VISION

Visualization is such a powerful tool. It allows you to internalize your passion and solidify what future experiences will feel like. Thinking through multiple aspects of your vision helps bring it to life. Ask yourself what type of leader you want to be. What challenges do you want to find solutions for, what kind of difference do you want to make, who will carry on your legacy? It's normal to feel excited, nervous, or even scared when you start internalizing your visions, but know that the first step to making your dreams become reality is gaining clarity on what you want your future to look like. If you are unclear about your vision, any future will do. You have to be fully engaged in order to manifest what it is you really want. Use your passions to fuel your unique vision. Be intentional in the way you think and speak about your dreams. Positive thoughts will attract more positive outcomes; this power needs to be harnessed when you begin bringing your vision to life. Stretch yourself. Don't worry about the *"how"* when you begin visualizing; focus on the *"why"* and the feelings associated with living in greater alignment with your truth.

SET *S.M.A.R.T.* GOALS

After understanding your passion and internalizing your vision, begin taking the necessary steps to make it a reality. One of the best ways to do so is by leveraging *S.M.A.R.T.* (specific, measurable, attainable, relevant, time-bound) goals. While *S.M.A.R.T.* goals are not new, they still remain effective in guiding behaviors when followed-through with regularity. Executing them, not merely *"setting and forgetting"* is what separates great leaders from the rest. This will require you to revisit your *S.M.A.R.T.* goals habitually to ensure your day-to-day activities are aligned to your long-term vision. If your aim in life is to leverage your passion to realize your vision, you need to take goal setting seriously. This doesn't mean that your goals cannot be adapted. In fact, you should be adapting goals as needed to ensure they are still relevant to your situation. Goals are not meant to be arduous, they are meant to be supportive. Make them visible and make them work for you. Realizing your vision depends on it.

HOLD YOURSELF ACCOUNTABLE

No person on earth has more control in helping you achieve your dreams than you do. You owe it to yourself to put your best foot forward each and every day. This doesn't mean that you need to be perfect or work yourself into the ground. What it does mean is that you need to find the willpower to follow through on your goals when challenges arise. This is especially true when you find yourself procrastinating. Find the willpower within to swallow the frog (i.e. do the thing you don't want to do, but know you have to). Fight that little voice in your head justifying all the reasons why tomorrow is better than today. By doing so, you will immediately start feeling better because you will be making progress toward your goals. Remember to be honest with yourself—you know when you have the capacity to step up and when you need a break. Listen to your intuition. Don't beat yourself up over not achieving every goal exactly the way you set out to. Be kind to yourself, things in life rarely go exactly how we think they will go initially. Instead, focus on progress over perfection. Keep chipping away one day at a time, and eventually, you will wake up in awe realizing that you've achieved the vision you set for yourself.

In its simplest form, leadership development is a constant ebb and flow of fishing and snagging. Deciding to *F.I.S.H.* will undoubtedly come with snagging on situations or blind spots you never knew existed. Learning how to *S.N.A.G.* with grace will allow you to learn the lessons you need to learn in order to continue to *F.I.S.H.* Great coaches leverage this mindset to help their coachees break through to new heights. Your job is to make it clear to the anglers you bring on your boat—in order to *F.I.S.H.*, you must be prepared to *S.N.A.G.*

F.I.S.H.   The Ebb and Flow of Meaningful Growth   S.N.A.G.

CHAPTER 5

Honor Their Catch

Celebrate and Find Fulfillment in the Successes of Others

"Leaders are best when people barely know they exist, when their work is done, their aim fulfilled, the people will say: we did it ourselves."

-Lao Tzu

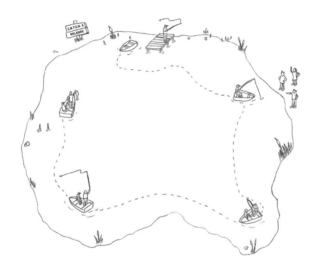

Leadership Constructs Discussed in *Honor Their Catch*
Vicarious Happiness • Humility
Losing the Need to Compare • Learning from Others

"*Fish on,*" Bob said in his cool and calm-tempered voice. My first reaction was one of excitement as I quickly reeled in my line to see what Bob had fighting at the end of his. It had been a few hours since I lost my fish and Bob and I were starting to feel the pressure to stay competitive in the tournament. This new bite was a breath of fresh air on an otherwise seemed suffocating day. As Bob carefully retrieved his fish, I grabbed the net, ready to assist in any way I could. As the smallmouth surfaced, I noticed the beautiful bronze color, dark vertical stripes, and signature red eyes. This truly was a beautiful fish, and one of good size too. With a swift swing of the net, I secured Bob's catch and we both looked at one another with new-found hope. Two quality fish were in the livewell, and there was still hope we could reach our limit of five before the day was over.

After the initial excitement began to fade from Bob's latest fish, a dark thought crept into my head as I started comparing my own contributions to those of Bob's. He had already produced two fish and all I had was a pit in my stomach. I was glad Bob caught the fish, but couldn't help feeling a little jealous or even worse—inadequate. This led me to begin thinking that maybe I wasn't a good enough angler to be fishing in this tournament with Bob. After all, he was the president of the club and I had just recently gotten back into fishing. Searching for something, anything to make myself feel a little better, I tried convincing myself that the smallies in this lake were different from the ones I used to catch on the Maquoketa River in my hometown of Cascade, IA. Their color, size, and habitat looked so much different, not to mention the lure and method we were using to catch them. I started victimizing myself, letting a dark downward spiral of comparison kick in.

As we continued fishing the same area, it was only a matter of minutes before Bob pulled out another fish! This fish was a little smaller than the last, but still qualified as a keeper and would add to our overall bag. We now had three of our five fish, and I wanted more than anything to help contribute by catching at least one of the last two.

Every catch is special. It connects us to something bigger than ourselves. It serves to teach us something new and reminds us to appreciate the small things in life. Honoring the catch humbles the soul, quiets the ego, and promotes feelings of happiness in ourselves and those around us. Life is short. And no catch should be taken for granted, no matter how big or small.

As far back as I can remember, I've always had an affinity for fish. Perhaps it's the result of being born a Pisces? Or maybe it was the family I was born into? Regardless of the source, my passion for all things fishing was alive and kicking at a very young age. As I grew, fishing, and everything related to it, began opening my mind to a whole new world of aquatic curiosity. I remember being fascinated by many fish-related quandaries. *How could fish breathe underwater?* I used to think to myself: *What did they eat? When did they sleep?* As time went on, some of the questions I asked became a little more sophisticated: *Would fish refuse to bite on the same lures they had previously been caught on? Could fish find their way back home, if they were released back into the water at a different spot within the same lake? How long would it take a fish to strike something new after having just been caught and released? Were big fish more intelligent or just more aggressive?* The list goes on and on, but there was one question that never really crossed my mind until much later in life: *How long do fish live?*

While working at the University of Iowa Water Plant as an undergraduate student, I was fortunate enough to have been led by a couple of supervisors who were as passionate about fishing as I was. I remember one of them sharing with me that a fully-matured fish, such as a largemouth bass, could live up to 20 years. At first, I had a hard time believing this, because, at the time, I myself was only 20 years old. Trying to wrap my head around the fact that some of the fish I caught were nearly my own age blew my mind. Reflecting on this new knowledge, I found myself fast-forwarding through the major events in my life—the places I had seen, the people I had met—and couldn't help but wonder what events the fish I actively pursued had encountered within the same time span. When you pause to think about it, it's truly remarkable how any fish survives the test of time and grows into a creature of beauty.

While it's tough to know the exact odds, some experts have estimated that for every 10,000 largemouth bass spawned, roughly 5-10 make it to adulthood (Russell, 2014). Give or take, that is equivalent to a 0.1% survival rate from birth. Take a second to think about that the next time you pose for a picture with your new friend. Your photogenic companion has survived all the elements, avoided predators, and foraged enough food to grow into a healthy adult able to reproduce the next generation of its kin. Surviving, however, is only part of the equation. The other part includes the odds associated with an angler being in the right place at the right time, using the right lure and approach, securing a good hook set, and not losing the fish in the retrieval process. When you account for all these variables, it's pretty extraordinary how unique each catch really is.

With this in mind, take a moment to think about how remarkable it is to have *"caught"* some of the great leaders in your life. You are one in eight billion (probably more) people in this world. Unless you are some kind of networking phenom, my guess is you will interact with far less than 0.1% (8,000,000) of the people that make up the world's population. Realistically, you have probably only crossed paths with a handful or two of people you would be willing to call great leaders. Each one likely teaching you something valuable on your journey. When you pause to think about it, it's nothing short of a miracle that you have connected with these special people in your life. I encourage you to keep this perspective in mind throughout your career. Each person that catches you, and you them, is something worth honoring. Never take it for granted.

Every Catch Is Special

The thrill of the catch is what continuously keeps leaders and anglers coming back for more. The catch—literally and metaphorically—can be somewhat addictive. The excitement of possibilities and the unpredictable nature of outcomes is what keeps life so interesting. The ongoing pursuit of positive reinforcement (e.g. a new sale, a new acquaintance, a trophy fish) occurs on a variable schedule, meaning that no fixed set of hours, phone calls, or casts, can guarantee you a meaningful catch. This is one of the main reasons why every catch should be honored.

If you are like me, at some point or another, you may have wondered why certain behaviors are more addictive than others. Take, for example, gambling at a casino, or for the avid angler, having to call it quits at dusk. The reason it can be so difficult to finally quit is the prospect that the next card dealt or cast thrown out could be *"the one,"* which is a psychological bias referred to as the *gambler's fallacy*. Regardless if you currently have a *"hot hand"* or are *"due for a good hand"* because of past misfortunate, your brain can trick itself into agreeing with the *"just one more"* logic. The reason is simple—we can't predict the future and there will always be a *"what if"* component associated with the pursuit of your next catch. The goal, however, should be to strive for an ongoing balance between the pursuit of new catches while still honoring the ones you've already caught.

For some anglers, fishing is more than just fishing, it's a spiritual experience. There is something magical about looking down into the eyes of a fish you just brought out of the water. The moment connects you to something greater than yourself. It prompts deep thoughts about the meaning of life and humanity's place in the world. The therapeutic act of casting and retrieving in a harmonious environment is truly blissful. Tranquility and adventure, all wrapped into one, rejuvenates the soul. Add the unexpected tug of a line, and it's easy to see how so many people become devoted disciples of the sport. Immersed in a state of flow, anglers arrive at new insights about themselves and the world they live in. There is a great sense of accomplishment and an overwhelming level of gratitude associated with catching and releasing an animal back into the wild. This beautiful balance of excitement and meaningful reflection also exists in leadership but it requires a high level of awareness and deep appreciation for each step of the *C.A.T.C.H. & Release.*

Although the thrill of the catch may never seem to get old, it does evolve over time. I am no longer that little boy yelling, *"Look at me! I got one, I got one, I GOT ONE!"* Instead, I have learned how to keep my composure until a fish has been landed, which is usually followed by a smile, fist bump, and some expressive words of excitement to my fellow co-anglers. After a quick picture and release, I purposely try to recall the exact circumstances and actions that were taken to entice the bite. For those interested around me, I offer to share advice based on my recent catch. As I've matured as an angler, I have found joy in sharing fishing secrets with others. I have begun to find that openly sharing the keys to my successes feels a lot better than withholding knowledge out of a fear that others will abuse it. Staying true to my word, I encourage you to check out a section titled *My Fishing Secrets* at the end of this book to learn more about my favorite fishing and leadership secrets.

Over time I have come to realize that setting others up for success brings me greater joy than catching fish myself. I want to spark that same passion, understanding, and appreciation for fishing in others that I experience myself. Words cannot describe the fulfillment I experience when I hear, *"I GOT ONE!"* from a new angler I just shared my secrets with. Every chance I get to connect someone to the passion I have for both fishing and leadership—I take. I feel that there are very few things in life better than knowing you played a part in creating a positive experience for another. Setting aside your own ego, removing the need for recognition, and eliminating feelings of jealousy when others succeed are all keys to honoring their catch, and honoring their catch is key to leadership.

The 5th step in the *C.A.T.C.H. & Release* Model is centered around a leader's ability to display humility and find joy in the successes of others. It requires leaders to stop measuring their own success compared to the successes of others and to shift their mindset from one of envy to one of appreciation. There should be no feelings of resentment in the heart of a leader who has groomed other leaders to surpass even their own ability. This point is vital and requires using the *Hooks of Honor* in order to secure the last step of the *C.A.T.C.H.*

THE HOOKS OF HONOR

Hook #1: Vicarious Happiness

Experiencing positive emotions through the happiness and success of others.

Early on in my career, I was fortunate enough to have a leader show me the power of vicarious happiness. He genuinely cared about sparking joy in others which also elevated his own mood in return. Although this leader dealt with a great deal of pressure in his day-to-day life, he made it a priority to fully engage in the happiness and excitement of others. As a small business owner, I'm sure that anxious thoughts about cash flow, staying competitive in the market, and fulfilling his vision consumed a significant portion of his mind; yet, even with all the pressures of leading his business, he was able to immerse himself at any given moment in the excitement and happiness of others. There was never a birthday, promotion, or major business accomplishment that went unnoticed. He always carved out time to celebrate the happiness of his employees. He sincerely listened, asked thoughtful questions, and made team members feel special in the moment. The laughter, happiness, and success of the team brought out the best in that leader. He mirrored their happiness, resulting in a warm, positive, and supportive environment. Even when some team members decided to leave the organization for new opportunities, he was able to share in their excitement and showed gratitude for their service. As difficult as it was to see people leave the company he built, he knew that resentment and bitterness would not help him in the future. One day I asked him how he was able to always be so happy for others. He told me, *"If you can't be happy for others, you will never be truly happy yourself."* At the time, I probably didn't fully appreciate this perspective, but as I reflect over the years, his advice has really grown on me and influenced the way I view leadership. I have come to realize that being present, happy, and appreciative of others during the special times in their lives helps build stronger relationships and more fulfillment in my own life. Unfortunately, leaders can sometimes be triggered by others' happiness causing them to compare and feel insecure about their own well-being, resulting in the projection of negativity. This feeling of resentment can happen to any leader—after all—leaders are human too. Can you relate to a time when someone else's success made you bitter or produced doubts in yourself. You may have thought to yourself, *things always seem to work out for them*, or *they always get lucky; why can't it ever be that easy for me?* Even in those trying moments, I challenge you to sincerely wish others well. There are no limits to happiness. Just because someone else experiences good fortune doesn't mean there is any less fortune for you to obtain. Happiness breeds more happiness if you allow it to do so. As a leader, you play a significant role in how you can make others, and, ultimately yourself feel. Challenge yourself to find new ways to celebrate the successes of others—you may be surprised by how quickly it can change your own outlook.

If You Can't Be Happy For Others, You'll Never Be Happy Yourself

Demonstrating vicarious happiness is especially important for leaders to display in the digital world we now find ourselves living in. It's far too easy to become triggered by the posts we see on social media. Whether someone we know just bought their dream home, was promoted, or found out they are expecting a child, try celebrating their happiness instead of allowing it to make you feel triggered. When I started writing this book, I can't tell you how many posts I saw on LinkedIn about other people who had successfully launched books. At first, it was hard for me to be truly happy for those who had already achieved what it was I was setting out to do. I thought, *who am I to try and write a book*, and *of course they're successful but what about me?* However, practicing what I preach, I started liking posts whenever I saw someone else's success. The second I hit the like button and decided to honor their success, my thoughts shifted. The bitterness or jealousy subsided, and I was able to move on without letting that potential trigger impact me the rest of the day. I can't emphasize how healing it's been to let go of my ego and truly celebrate the happiness of others. Remember that celebrating others' happiness has the power to generate more happiness when you allow it to ripple.

Hook #2: Humility
Displaying modesty and humbleness.

Humility serves as a stage to showcase others. It's the great platform leaders discreetly assemble with the intention of recognizing the talents of those around them. Instead of trying to stand in the center of the stage they built, great leaders seek to operate the spotlight. With great satisfaction, they shine a light on those who deserve it most. Far more valuable than gaining compliments is the mastery of how to dish them out. Great leaders know this, it's how they build cultures where people stay inspired and hungry for growth. While it's not always easy, this skill is definitely worthwhile for all leaders to learn.

A desire for acceptance and recognition are two powerful ingredients of the human condition. Humility requires a leader to tame the impulsive appetite of the ego seeking constant praise. Inevitably, there will be times when you don't get the recognition you think you deserve, and other times you feel unworthy of the recognition you do receive. Regardless of the situation, you must make a choice about the type of leader you wish to become. This will require a great deal of self-control and an ability to see the bigger picture. As one seeking to become a great leader, will you let your actions be driven by hubris or humility?

Believe me when I tell you that boastful leaders who choose to talk up their own accomplishments as a means to inspire others are far less effective in building comradery than leaders who display humility. It sounds so basic, but you would be surprised by the number of leaders in organizations who—consciously or unconsciously—feel the unsolicited need to project stories of their own successes onto others. Bragging to others—whether knowingly or not—acts as a barrier between yourself and those you wish to influence. All leaders have room to grow, no matter how influential or well-known they may be. Knowing this, embrace the opportunity you have as a leader to lift others up by prioritizing the recognition of their accomplishments over your own. Build their confidence instead of victimizing yourself by thinking of all the ways you should be praised. When you do encounter success, resist the urge to gloat. Instead, remove yourself from the spotlight. You are not the center of the universe, but you possess the opportunity to make others feel like they are.

Unavoidably, there will be days when you, as a leader, feel like you aren't receiving the recognition you deserve for your team's success. As tempting as it may be to want to take credit for grooming or influencing others, refrain from doing so. This is their moment, honor their catch, regardless of the role you think you played in it. If you are leading effectively, others will pick up on the role you played. You don't need the recognition; it's just your ego telling you that you do. People are motivated to go above and beyond when they work with a leader who praises their contributions over their own. Let your actions speak louder than your words. Never underestimate the power of lifting others up. Your team will show their appreciation through their productivity and willingness to go the extra mile. Your praise and recognition in them will propel them through the challenges they face. Even if no one tells you, you should feel good about the impact you have made and your ability to role model humility to others.

You Don't Need The Recognition, It's Just Your Ego Telling You That You Do

Back in 2010, I remember taking a co-worker from the pizza shop I worked at fishing for the very first time. I vividly remember providing him with all the gear, intel, and fishing spots where he could catch his first fish. I tied on the best lure I had for him and gave him first dibs to cast at the spots I knew had produced fish in the past. My friend had a lot of success that day, and I felt good about helping him create some new memories; yet, he failed to see it as clearly as me. He made some remarks that day that really rubbed me the wrong way. For example, every time he caught a fish, he asked how many I had caught. Every time he caught a larger fish than I, he reminded me with some wise-guy remark about how well the new guy was doing in comparison to the so-called *"pro."* I don't think he was intentionally trying to be mean, but he was blind to the fact that my role was imperative to his success that day. As bad as I wanted to remind him that the only reason he was having so much success was because I had spent hours gaining knowledge of the lake and was willing to share it with him; I held my tongue. After a deep breath, I took solace acknowledging the role I played in providing him with a memorable first fishing experience. I tried my best to honor his catch that day, even though it tested my patience in a big way.

Humility, as powerful as it can be for a leader, does have a downside if overused. There is a risk in being overly humble. Strive for a balance in being able to accept praise periodically while still focusing your efforts on lifting others up. It's okay to accept a compliment and speak highly of yourself on occasion. Your team looks up to you and they will expect you to be recognized for your contributions from time to time. Just remember to show class and practice good judgment when you do. More times than not, choose to operate the spotlight rather than taking a bow from center stage.

Hook #3 : Losing the Need to Compare

Avoiding the need to measure personal success against the successes of others.

Measuring success is key to growth in any area of your life. Without measurement, you might as well be navigating your journey blindfolded. There's a chance you may stumble onto success here or there. You know the saying, *"Even a blind squirrel finds a nut once in a while;"* but, if you are really hungry for success and interested in finding it more than every once in a while, you'll need the appropriate metrics to guide you.

The first step to measuring your success is to rid yourself of the mindset that your success is determined by how it stacks up against others. As strong as the urge is to compare yourself to others, you must resist. It provides little benefit to your growth in the long run and can end up costing you years of misery trying to dig yourself out of a dark comparison hole. Measuring your success compared to others is problematic because it's solely determined by the upward or downward comparisons you make. For example, let's say you begin feeling really good about yourself after comparing your success to your less-motivated sibling (downward comparison) who still lives with your parents. You trick yourself into thinking that you have accomplished more than them and, at a minimum, have the dignity to live on your own. However, the moment you start to gloat, you see online that your college classmate who took all the same classes as you was just promoted to a role at a Future 100 company two levels higher than the one you currently hold (upward comparison). Suddenly you start feeling ashamed, convincing yourself that you are a complete failure because you still work for an organization no one has ever heard of, not to mention that you have no clue when you're up for your next promotion.

Your brain is powerful, and making unhealthy social comparisons can trick you into trying to measure your own success by using someone else's measuring stick. Depending on your comparison, whether upward or downward, you may feel high and mighty one second and down in the dumps the next. Going through this pattern all day is not productive nor helpful as a leader.

Your Success Should Never Be Measured By Someone Else's Measuring Stick

The concept of losing the need to compare has only grown in recent years with the increasing role social media plays in our lives. Comparing our lives to the lives portrayed by our connections online only adds fuel to the fire. For a number of years now, psychological studies have begun identifying the extent to which social comparisons online can negatively influence a person's self-esteem (Vogel, Rose, Roberts, & Eckles, 2014). A contributing factor to this negative effect is the tendency for most people to post content that makes them look good to the public. Instead of seeing everything behind the scenes, we typically only see the positive highlights in people's lives and make comparisons based on our own everyday life experiences. Think of your own posting habits. When was the last time you posted a picture or an accomplishment that was anything less than flattering? As people mindlessly scroll through their feeds, their perception of reality is greatly distorted. It's important to keep this in mind and strengthen your awareness of how social media comparison, or any type of comparison, makes you feel. Many of the comparisons you make are likely unfair to begin with and will consequently inhibit your ability to lead effectively. Avoid the tendency to inflate your ego, or be triggered by comparing your success to others. Instead, strive for progress using your personal history as the measuring stick to gauge your current and future success. Only you can truly define and measure your success—looking elsewhere will hinder your development and likely just make you end up feeling shitty.

Hook #4 - Learning from Others
The ability to apply lessons learned from others to one's own life.

There is a saying by an unknown author that states, *"A smart person learns from their own mistakes, but a wise person learns from the mistakes of others."* This powerful quote combines two key components of leadership: the ability to learn from failures, and the ability to learn from others. While we often think of wisdom as an individual trait, it's actually the collective learning of many applied by one. Before acquiring any wisdom, one must possess a willingness to truly listen to others on their path to enlightenment.

Listening can be one of the most difficult skills to master in a lifetime. Several inhibiting factors can negatively influence one's ability to listen: efforts to multi-task, a lack of sincere empathy, or prematurely offering a solution, just to name a few. True listening goes far beyond simply hearing an individual—it requires a person to pause their own personal agenda and create the mental space to allow their counterpart to communicate a message. This can be incredibly challenging for leaders at first, especially those accustomed to directing action instead of absorbing it. So often leadership is thought of as the outward ability to deliver a magnificent speech that inspires thousands, coach someone through a monumental challenge, or make a strategic business decision resulting in exponential growth. Unfortunately, listening is often overlooked as a predominant leadership skill. Perhaps this is because it's viewed as a passive behavior, or because it's not the way leadership is often portrayed in movies. Ironically listening, not speaking, is the foundation for all development, both in oneself and others.

There is an ancient story that has been passed on through history known as the *Teacup Story* that I'd like to share with you. While many variations of this story exist online and in books, the message is always the same. The story goes something like this...

A long time ago, there was a wise Zen master respected by all. People would come far and wide to soak up the master's wisdom and become more enlightened in the ways of Zen. Even though the master was so sought after, he rarely turned anyone away.

One day, a man of great status and wealth came to visit the master. The man visiting was authoritarian by nature, expecting that people listen and obey him. On that day, the man came to ask the master to teach him the ways of Zen.

With a smile, the Zen master suggested the two of them discuss the matter over a cup of tea. When the tea was ready, the master began to pour the tea into the man's cup. As the man continued to talk, the master continued to pour. Before long, the tea began to pour beyond the rim of the man's cup, over the table, and onto the clothes of the man. The man shouted to the master to stop, asking him if he could not see that the cup was full.

The Zen master stopped and smiled. He told the man, "You are like this teacup, so full that nothing more can be added. Visit me again when your cup is empty, and your mind has room to grow."

Remember this story throughout your own leadership career. If you truly want to grow and discover new ways to improve yourself, you must create space for new wisdom to be poured into you. It requires humility, self-control, and an appetite for silence in order to listen to yourself and those around you.

Building on concepts outlined in Chapter 2, *Attract Diverse Anglers*, learning from others who possess diverse experiences will greatly expedite your leadership development. A key component of learning from others goes beyond just listening—it requires the application of new learnings to one's own life. In the leadership field, there is a common developmental framework referred to as the *70-20-10 Model*. This model is largely used for development planning, and it suggests that 70% of your development should come from personal experiences, 20% learning from others (e.g. coaches, mentors), and 10% from formal learning methods, such as reading or training courses. There is no question that the greatest learning you will gain as a leader will be from your own personal experiences (i.e. trial and error). The key to accelerating your development though will be how quickly you apply the learnings you acquire from others into your own experiences. Instead of letting great coaching sessions, seminars you attend, or books you read (the 20-10 respectively) be forgotten, soak them in and find ways to apply them! Many of the lessons shared from those sources are the mistakes of others, which shouldn't become your own if you seek to become a wise leader.

Having gone through the *C.A.T.C.H.* portion of the *C.A.T.C.H. & Release* Model, my hope is that you have begun to think about leadership in some new ways. I also hope you've allowed yourself the opportunity to openly reflect on the constructs you exhibit as strengths and those you still need to work on in the future.

In full transparency, until my last review of this book, I failed to honor the catch of someone who is very important to me. Much of what I have shared with you in this chapter and the next is a credit to my wife

Alisha. She opened my eyes to new ways of thinking which have laid the foundation for many of the lessons outlined in the *Release*. Let my oversight serve as a reminder that practicing this model is an ongoing journey, even for yours truly.

CHAPTER 6

Release

Self-Reflect, Let Go, and Show Gratitude for What Matters Most

"Fishing provides that connection with the whole living world. It gives you the opportunity of being totally immersed, turning back into yourself in a good way. A form of meditation, some form of communion with levels of yourself that are deeper than the ordinary self"

-TED HUGHES

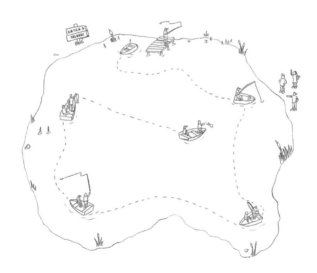

Leadership Constructs Discussed in the *Release*
Self-Reflection • Self-Forgiveness • Practicing Mindfulness
Optimistic Mindset • Learning How to Unlearn

Zero. The number of fish I was able to land that painful day on Lake St. Clair. As we decided to fire up the big motor and head back to the boat ramp for weigh-in, the negativity sunk in. How could I have spent all day fishing and have nothing to show for it? Without Bob's three keepers, it would have been a complete disaster. All I kept thinking was how terrible of a fisherman I was. *Just another fake, wannabe angler, who didn't deserve to be on the team. It was my own fault that I missed that fish. The team would have been better off without me.* Here I was proudly representing the University of Iowa at the onset of the tournament, only to feel like a complete failure at its conclusion. Another Big Ten Classic in the books, and this time a big fat skunk left a mental stench I couldn't shake.

After weighing in our bag of three fish, Bob and I posed for a picture. If only Bob had three hands, I wouldn't have had to held up his third catch of the day. To make matters worse, my left hand remained empty, serving as a reminder of my missed opportunity. Without a second fish to hold, I desperately tried to grasp any kind of lesson I could clinch onto from that day on Lake St. Clair.

(Big Ten Classic 2009 Lake St. Clair, MI)

Our team ended up placing in the middle of the pack. To little surprise, the local Big Ten team, Michigan State University, took first place. They were fishing the same technique as us, they just had more experience and better-marked GPS locations. After the photo, Bob and I admired 'our' (his) fish one last time as we released them back into their natural habitat. Never before had I felt so inadequate in my fishing ability. Although Bob was very supportive and sympathetic to the fact that it was a tough day on the water for most anglers, I was still overcome by disappointment. Even worse, we had an 8-hour car ride home, allowing me to ruminate over the situation that much longer. Whatever the lesson was for me to learn that day, it sure came at an agonizing price. Even though those fish were released back into the water that day, a splinter would remain caught between my ears for years to come.

———

Take a deep breath, hold it in, now let it out. Pause in this moment, build some awareness to how you're feeling right now. Where are you at in your mind, body, and soul? Regardless of how great or inadequate you may feel, take one more deep breath, fill your lungs all the way up, and let it all go. You've made it to the *Release*.

When I set out to write this book, I knew that this chapter—compared to all others—would be the most unique for readers. Most of the concepts and ideas that are discussed in the *Release* are not traditional leadership concepts. With that being said, I firmly believe that your ability to regularly practice the *Release* is what will make the greatest difference in your leadership ability over your lifetime. In the introduction, I mentioned that some elements of leadership have stood the test of time (and will continue to stand the test of time), while other less common elements will need to be honed to navigate the challenges brought on by leading in the digital age.

This chapter provides advice on how leaders can combat the substantial pressure that leading today creates. The focus is to help leaders find new techniques to recharge and rediscover the best version of themselves by removing obstacles and negativity that impact their success. Come with an open mind, break the cycle, and learn how to embrace the *Release*.

Here's a deep question for you to ponder: What matters most in your life? Is it your health, wealth, relationships, faith, career, or simply just being happy? I realize it's a difficult question to answer and there are no right or wrong responses, but try to answer it honestly. I also want you to ask yourself when was the last time you dedicated adequate time to think about it? The reason I bring this up is that not knowing what you want, or what's most important in your life, is a surefire way to unhappiness.

Perhaps you already know the answer to the question above, but fall into the trap of convincing yourself that you have to sacrifice one priority in order to be successful in another? When one area of your life seems to be going swimmingly, does another appear to be falling apart? Does that logic always hold true; does it have to? Unfortunately, life can sometimes feel like an endless chase for fulfillment. A twisted game of musical chairs, shifting and reshuffling priorities whenever one area in our lives feels out of whack with the other. Constant feelings of being inadequate and always operating behind the eight-ball can lead to stress, burnout, and paralyzing anxiety. You know deep down that a better balance exists for you, but where and how is it attained?

Finding a balance isn't easy, and it doesn't come naturally to many leaders. Society has largely prevailed in programming us to believe that we should operate our lives like machines—striving for perfection, in every area, all the time. We often feel tremendous amounts of pressure to keep our power switch locked in the *"on"* position even when our minds and bodies need to be powered down. Chasing one thing after another, we become frustrated, hopeless, and burnt out as our lives pass us by. We try to squeeze as much out of every minute of every day because our minds have become conditioned with phrases like *"time is money"* and *"the clock's ticking,"* which only creates more anxiety and a constant state of being stretched too thin. It's a real epidemic, one where we relentlessly drain our batteries beyond the point of recovery by trying to accommodate everything we (and society) asks of ourselves. This overstretched and misaligned state becomes notably apparent when one day we wake up and realize we are operating our lives on autopilot. Suddenly, our interactions become robotic and only one word can prove our worth: *busy*. How was the weekend? *"busy."* How is work? *"busy."* How's the family? *"Good but busy!"* These mindless, zombie-like responses are indicative of how many people go through the motions of their lives, knowing full-heartedly that being *"busy"* doesn't justify self-worth or happiness—yet we've conditioned ourselves to feel shame if we don't respond with *busy* when asked how life is going. This unsustainable mode of operation often leaves us feeling at a loss—like there is never enough time or energy to truly accomplish what we want. Instead of feeling happy and fulfilled with our lives, we keep chasing the next carrot, shiny toy, or title to serve as the token for our success. This inner battle we wage on ourselves, between what we know is best for our well-being and what is best for the machine, never seems to end.

As a leader, I'm asking you to make an important decision: continue operating as part of the *"busy"* zombie apocalypse, or stop the madness by regaining control of your state of mind. And yes, deciding not to decide is still a decision, something every leader needs to be reminded of from time to time. If you do, however, desire to make a change, start by examining the root causes of your autopilot responses. Question why you continue convincing yourself that your current mode of operation is the only option you have. Is it possible to say no to things? Will the sun still come up in the morning if you carve a little time out for yourself to recharge? Will answering questions openly and honestly (showing some vulnerability) really change the perception others have of you? I ask you, for your own health and wellness, to make a conscious decision to take back the one thing that was yours from the beginning—your peace of mind.

Somewhere on this human journey, we lost a fundamental connection to ourselves, the present moment, and the mental perspective that promotes balance and sustainability. You could point to monumental shifts in history—the industrial revolution, the rise of consumerism, or rapid advancements in technology as the predecessors—but regardless of the culprit, a new norm has been established. One in which people operate at a single speed—full-throttle. While we know it's not sustainable, many continue to play the part until small complications in our lives manifest into major issues affecting our physical, emotional, and mental well-being.

Somewhere Along The Way, We Lost A Fundamental Connection To Ourselves

To reduce the wear and tear on ourselves, we need to learn how to kick this single-speed into a new gear, one that is more sustainable and yields greater results over time. A gear that forces us to slow down before we speed up. One that allows us to collect ourselves and become more intentional with our cognitive resources. The new name of the game is learning how to sprint, at the right time, in a nimble way. Learning how to do this will delineate a leader's sustainable success from their unsustainable burnout. Leaders who embrace this change will outshine their counterparts who still believe operating in full-throttle 24/7 is the only way to build a lasting legacy. But, in order to sprint, one first must let go of any baggage, added stress, and unnecessary complexity in their lives. This requires leaders to learn how to *Release*.

The 6th step of the *C.A.T.C.H. & Release* Model relates to a leader's ability to find gratitude, balance, and longevity during their journey. The *Release* helps combat burnout, negativity, and the limiting beliefs that surface as a leader. The *C.A.T.C.H.* and the *Release* have a symbiotic relationship, meaning both elements go hand in hand. They should not be thought of as mutually exclusive, but rather as a tandem that enhances one another. If the *C.A.T.C.H.* is thought of as the process to develop future leaders, think of the *Release* as the process to sustain the energy and mental plasticity in order to continue the *C.A.T.C.H.* over time.

Leadership is not its strongest with one or the other, but with an ongoing equilibrium between the two.

The role of the *Release* in leadership dawned on me several years back while fishing with my family. We developed a ritual derived from the popular show in the mid-2000s on the Discovery Channel, called *Deadliest Catch*. Shortly after the launch of *Deadliest Catch*, a new segment, called *After the Catch*, was created. In the show, *After the Catch*, competing crab fishermen on the Bering Sea would get together after their expeditions and reflect on their experiences. Regardless of who won that season of *Deadliest Catch*, there were lessons learned, memories made, and laughs to be had. The segment did a great job of reinforcing the importance of self-reflection and continuous improvement. Personally, I found it just as entertaining as the footage of the catches themselves. Leveraging this idea, my family and I began making sure to prioritize time after our fishing experiences to chat and share memories. The process has allowed us to decompress, appreciate the experience, and soak in the new lessons we learned for future trips on the water. Over the years, I've learned to appreciate our *After the Catch*-like ritual just as much as the time spent fishing. Participating in conversations about different fishing patterns, weather conditions, and the thrilling catches we landed or lost never grows old to me. I think the common reason, (mentioned throughout this book) is that no two days on the water are ever exactly the same. There is no way to replicate all of the exact variables (e.g. weather, time of the year, water levels, fishing habitat, etc.) a specific fishing moment creates. Realizing this, I try to approach each experience on the water as a unique opportunity to learn something new and improve my overall skill set. This perspective helps me soak in both the lessons I have learned as well as the lessons I've learned from others. These deeply reflective moments are what I live for.

One day, around a bonfire with my family, it hit me—if leaders spent more time reflecting on ways to learn from their experiences and less time worrying about things they can't control, perhaps they would be happier and more productive. I thought to myself, *Why don't people make more of a conscious effort to learn from their experiences through reflection, better yet—why don't they prioritize sharing their experiences with others? Why do so many people continue putting up a facade, tricking themselves into thinking that they will just be happier whenever that next thing happens?* These questions led me to start thinking of the concept of the *Release* through the eyes of a leader.

When you're a leader, no two days you experience will ever be the same. The people you interact with, your to-do list, and all the random thoughts that cross your mind are exclusive to that individual moment. The present moment truly is a unique gift. Learning how to seize it and continuously learn from it—regardless of the outcome—will greatly serve you in your journey.

Every leadership experience provides opportunities to *Release*— to deeply reflect, find gratitude, and discover inner peace with oneself. Learning how to maintain a balance and let go of what no longer serves you are lessons that will change your life. To unlock what resides deep inside of you requires a better understanding of how your thoughts, experiences, and behaviors create your current reality. This means that taking the next step forward sometimes actually means stopping in your tracks to come to terms with the steps you have taken in your past.

Throughout my consulting career, I've found that elements of the *Release* are often the most underrepresented topics in leadership development. Leaders and organizations tend to shy away from aspects of the *Release* because the elements tend to deal with deeply rooted beliefs, emotions, and experiences that are easier to avoid than work through. The reality, though, is that every day mental challenges have the potential to build up, some consciously and others subconsciously. If leaders are not intentional in identifying them and finding ways to work through them, these mental challenges can cause major roadblocks later in life. This mental work is extremely important to leadership, but still, it does not receive the same amount of 'airtime' as other popular leadership topics. Mental health topics increasingly find themselves left off the agenda during leadership discussions and seminars. In my experience, the physical health of a leader is even more widely discussed at programs than the mental health of a leader; perhaps, because mental health is more difficult to see, and certainly more challenging to discuss? Take a second to think about conversations you typically have with your coworkers, whether in the break room, parking lot, or even over instant messenger. Do you have more impromptu discussions on ways to improve your physical health (eating healthy, working out, sleeping better, etc.) than ways to improve your mental health (meditating, journaling, opening up to someone about a hardship, etc.)? The stigma around mental health is still alive and well, and it definitely impacts a leader's ability to lead, whether it's openly talked about or not. Keep in mind, you don't need to be diagnosed with a mental health disorder to start making mental health a priority in your life.

While it's likely that popular leadership training will continue focusing on more surface-level leadership concepts over discussing deep-rooted mental blocks, you don't have to. You get to control what you focus on as a leader, and what you focus on grows. If you take nothing else away from this book, I encourage you to explore what really resides below the tip of your leadership iceberg. Doing so will directly influence the way you behave as a leader, which can have a rippling impact on others. Once you fully understand the depths of your core, you will be able to lower the water surrounding the iceberg, allowing so much more of your authentic leadership to surface. This process begins when you recognize just how much your leadership ability is influenced by the mental patterns that reside in your mind.

THE PHYSICAL AND MENTAL ELEMENTS OF THE *RELEASE*

In the fishing community, practicing catch and release, or C&R, has helped preserve countless fisheries all over the world. This conscious effort made by millions of anglers every year to sustain the sport they love does not go unnoticed. The beauty of C&R is that over time it becomes a mindset, not just a rule to follow. When this shift occurs, the release of a fish doesn't feel like a void, but, instead, the creation of a new experience for a future soul.

In leadership, the physical *Release* symbolizes letting go of the individuals you have brought along on your boat throughout the *C.A.T.C.H.* Inevitability, the time comes for every master to let their apprentice go out into the world and own their truth. As much as we may want to stop time to protect the people we care about from failure and hardships, we must let others find their own way. As a leader following the *C.A.T.C.H. & Release*, find solace in knowing that you've equipped your fellow companions with the knowledge and experience they need to accomplish big things in this world. Like a parent watching a child grow, or a teacher guiding a student toward graduation, you too will need to release the leaders you've developed on your journey. After all, it's the only way they can carry on a legacy of their own.

One of the most difficult career decisions I had to make early on was deciding to leave the consulting company I started with after graduate school. During my time there, I built a lot of strong relationships with clients and coworkers, developed a nice skill set, and learned from hundreds of experiences I wouldn't have received in any other entry-level role. When I decided to move to California to take on my next career challenge, I still remember how my previous employer took the news. As a small business owner, he was initially taken aback by it, not in an angry way, but in a surprised one. He wanted to help, even though he knew he was going to be losing a valuable resource on his team. I remember telling him, *"Someday I want to do what you do, I want to build my own consulting and coaching firm."* As hard as it was for him to let me go, he understood. My path to greatness would require a different path than the one he had anticipated for me. Leaving on good terms and making it a priority to stay in touch afterward has boded well for both of us. Parting ways wasn't easy at first, and in some ways, it felt like a breakup, but today, we still both greatly respect and encourage one another to continue living out our dreams. Many of the leadership topics I write about in this book, I learned under his wing, and I am incredibly grateful for his trust in me at such a pivotal time in my career.

Coming to terms with the physical *Release* of those you have learned to care about can be challenging. It requires a healthy mindset, one that does not come without patience and practice. People will come and go in your life, and some departures will hurt more than others. But keep in mind that whenever someone is released from your boat, it opens up room for another person to come aboard.

As challenging as the physical *Release* can be, over time, people eventually find closure which is usually marked by a specific date—graduation, wedding, starting a new job, etc. Life goes on, people come and go—these are concepts most leaders can grow to accept in their lives. However, the mental *Release* (letting go of the thoughts, worries, and stories you tell yourself throughout your life) is not typically celebrated with some major event or send-off. Mental challenges tend to be more cyclical by nature, consisting of the ongoing mind games we continue to play in our heads. While people can avoid or neglect mental challenges for certain periods of time, they always come back—unless they are properly addressed. A simple example of a common mental challenge you or someone you know likely faces is having a healthy relationship with money. When a person has lived the majority of their life being told *"Money doesn't grow on trees!"* they likely have convinced themselves that—no matter what—there never will be enough. Even worse, they may experience extreme guilt, anxiety, or paralysis in their ability to make financial decisions out of a fear of disappointing others (e.g. parent, in-law, spouse, etc.). After all, the last thing this person would want is for someone to think they are spending their money foolishly. So, instead of working on changing this mindset, the individual continues to reinforce this deeply ingrained limiting belief through their actions. Even if this person temporarily suppresses their deeply rooted beliefs by going out and buying something nice, the guilt will resurface again and again until the mindset has fully shifted. It's not until the person makes a conscious decision to let go of the limiting belief that the pattern stops.

Ultimately, your goal should be to identify the mental patterns you currently have and determine which ones promote your well-being and which ones do not. Being mindful of your spending habits is a good thing, but it can be a double-edged sword if you feel like you are being deprived or guilt-ridden into behaving in ways that aren't aligned with your mental needs. Remember that if your head is not in a good place, nothing else will be. The mental *Release* is designed to help leaders learn how to let go of negative thoughts and beliefs that no longer serve them in their ability to lead. Your personal growth will be its strongest when you begin to fully accept yourself, change the negative stories you have been telling yourself, and learn how to move on in a productive way. Your thoughts paint your reality; learn how to use them to create your own masterpiece.

Have you ever wondered why some people seem to be more put together and happier than others? Perhaps someone comes to mind right now: a person who always seems to glow, someone who handles pressures with grace and tends to bring the best out in others. Would you say the person you are thinking of is generally happy? Do they have a positive outlook on life and refrain from being overly cynical when facing adversity? For the longest time, I wanted to believe people with these characteristics were either born that way or were just really good at faking how they really felt. Over the years, however, I have begun to see how flawed my initial assumptions were. I have noticed that positive people work hard at creating their disposition. They prioritize their happiness and the activities that promote it. Similar to other monumental accomplishments in life, whether academic, financial, or physical, happiness requires a conscious effort to achieve. It dawned on me, in life you have to know what you want, and then work really hard to go get it; so why would happiness be any different? As a leader, I encourage you to continually seek ways to improve your mental health, reduce stress, and find inner peace throughout your journey. The best part is, most of the support you need resides within yourself and it can be rediscovered through the *Release*.

Before we go into each element of the *Release*, it is important for you to understand what is, and is not, within your control. The great news is that there is a lot you can personally do to improve your outlook on life if you are willing to break certain mental cycles and explore new waters. Improvement begins when you start viewing your mental health through the same lens as you do your physical health: taking preventive measures and being proactive. Just as it doesn't make sense to wait until you are morbidly obese to start working out, it doesn't make sense to avoid taking control of your mental health until you reach the point of a breakdown. Great leaders make time to ensure their minds are in a good place. They fully understand the importance of making sure their head is on right before they tackle the challenges any given day throws at them. Unfortunately, some leaders continue to fall into the trap of masking their mental health deficiencies as mere stressors related to their job. While stress is an inevitable part of most leadership positions, it is important to understand the difference between stress and the deeply rooted beliefs that hinder your ability to lead. Perhaps your repetitive, unhealthy thoughts, are one of the main culprits of work stress in the first place?

Great Leaders Priortize Actions That Support Their Mental Health

At this point in the chapter, you are probably ready to just get on with it, but I must take one final moment to discuss a topic near and dear to my heart. As someone who has witnessed the pain and suffering of mental illness first hand, I want you to know that if there is ever a point in your life that you feel like you are drowning, losing all hope, and are in a dark and depressing place, please ask for help. Don't let your ego or pride get in the way, blocking you from what you truly need—connection and support. Suicide is a real problem. While it may not be talked about much, rates have risen by a staggering 33% since 1999, and now suicide is a top-ten cause of death in the U.S., according to the Center for Disease Control (CDC) (Godlasky & Dastagir, 2018). As a leader, or more importantly—a human being—there is no shame in asking for help when you need it. If fear of judgment is holding you back, know that most people will show compassion and empathy toward your situation because they have likely been there themselves. Throughout your life as a leader, people will come to you for support when they are in need. They will share some of their most insecure vulnerabilities with you, and you will feel grateful and honored that they found comfort in your council. When navigating the cold and dark waters of your own life, don't ever talk yourself into thinking that you are completely alone and that no one will want to listen to you because you're supposed to be strong and have all the answers. If you are reading this book, you understand the positive impact humans can have on one another. Don't ever tell yourself that you are too weak, stupid, or unfit to lead. There are people who genuinely care about you and believe in you. We will all go through dark points in our lives, times that seem so desperate and bleak that we don't want to continue on. Remember that in your darkest hour, there is still a light inside of you. A light that will someday shine bright again. A light that will spark passion in others and illuminate a path for their success. You have a purpose and an opportunity to work miracles in yourself and others. Don't let fear and doubt extinguish your light prematurely; you have a beacon to share with the world.

OK, I said my bit, it needed to be shared. Please do your part to break the mental health stigma and help those who are hurting from the inside out. For anyone seeking immediate support for themselves or another please call the U.S. National Suicide Prevention Lifeline 1-800-273-TALK (8255) to talk it out with a professional who understands.

LIFE JACKETS OF THE *RELEASE*

At various times in your career, you will find yourself needing a life jacket to keep your head above water. With leadership, and all its glory, comes the weight of responsibility. Heavy is the head that wears the crown, right? It's no secret—being a great leader is no easy task. It requires so much time, energy, and effort to get it right. Instead of showing an ounce of vulnerability, some leaders will let the pressures of life build up to the point that they cause serious complications. Even though this may seem like the norm in today's day and age, this doesn't need to be the case. Sustainability and longevity are just as important to leadership as any other element. Ask yourself: *What's the point of developing leadership skills if you aren't healthy enough to demonstrate them to others?* Going the extra mile, whatever the cost, is not always worth the reward. As I've said before, sometimes the juice is simply not worth the squeeze. Ideally, you should be practicing the *Release* prior to the point of mental exhaustion; but in any event, it's better late than never. On the water, it's best to secure your life jacket before your boat capsizes, but if you already find yourself in the water; it doesn't hurt to have someone throw you one. Each element of the *Release* can be thought of as just that—a life jacket keeping your head above water when the pressures of leadership weigh you down.

Life Jacket #1: Self-Reflection

Prioritizing time to think about one's own thoughts, behaviors, and impact.

If I was a gambling man, I would wager that at some point on your leadership journey, you've heard of the importance of self-reflection. I would be tempted to place an even higher wager on the prospect that you don't actively schedule a time to self-reflect on your weekly calendar. And, if I was feeling really lucky, I might even bet the farm that you don't even know where to begin when it comes to integrating a self-reflection regiment into your leadership practice. Now that I'm ahead in the chip count, let me cash in and explain why self-reflection is not something to gamble on when it comes to your own development.

Failing to make time to self-reflect greatly inhibits your ability to realize your full potential. Without an accurate understanding of your skill set and the experiences of your past, present, and future, you're essentially allowing your leadership boat to be blown in whichever direction the wind is gusting in on a given day. While it's true that learning through personal experience is the most effective learning method there is; the lessons themselves will not fully mature into deep-rooted learnings if you don't allow time to process and make sense of your experiences. Think of reflection as a sort of marinating process in which you are adding flavor and allowing time to breakdown the toughness of the learning. This process enhances the culinary experience and leads to a greater appetite to try new recipes in the future. As tempting as it may be to short-change yourself on the reflection process, don't do it! Treat self-reflection with the same devotion you do any other aspect of leadership and you will see the return in all facets of your life. While many leaders acknowledge the importance of self-reflection, some still have a hard time implementing reflective behaviors into their routine because they view it as counter-productive to achieving goals. The unfortunate truth is that self-reflection is still viewed as the antithesis of productivity by some, and the last thing these individuals want is to be seen as someone who is not always *"busy."* Opting-out of self-reflection, these leaders justify their actions by choosing to cross something else off their to-do list instead of investing time in themselves. Constantly running in circles, checking boxes, and feeling persistent anxiety to get something else done perpetuates these individuals to repeat the same mental mistakes over and over again.

When I boil it down, these are the primary reasons I believe self-reflection is avoided by some leaders:

1. It requires leaders to slow down.
2. Leaders must embrace the reality that they aren't perfect.
3. It requires leaders to re-examine what the patterns of events in their lives are telling them about themselves, which can dig up some deep-rooted emotions.
4. Leaders may fear judgment from others who do not prioritize self-reflection themselves.

Despite all the reasons one can think of to avoid self-reflection, it's often the work leaders need to do from the inside out that pays the greatest dividends in the long run. You have a choice to make: start prioritizing self-reflection in your own leadership practice or continue going through the motions of life mindlessly.

On the flip side, it's important to acknowledge that too much of anything, self-reflection included, can be a bad thing. Self-reflecting in obsessive and non-constructive ways can be detrimental to your leadership development. If you are the type of leader who over-analyzes every minor detail throughout your day, you run the risk of paralyzing your own ability to lead. Self-reflection, in many ways, can be thought of as the process of looking into a mirror. Some leaders can spend all day holding it up examining themselves, which can be unhealthy and even narcissistic. It is important for self-reflection to be constructive and balanced, happening periodically and with intention.

At its core, self-reflection is composed of two basic principles: perception and reality. How you think about yourself as a leader (perception) and how you actually come across as a leader (reality). The closer you bridge the gap between your own perception and your reality, the more effective you will be as a leader. If you never make time to check the alignment between the two, you may be missing out on powerful insights to help you lead more effectively. Here are some general guidelines to improve your ability to self-reflect in a constructive manner.

Write It Down...

Self-reflection is strongest when you write down the lessons you've learned. Document both the strengths and development areas you identify in your leadership practice. It's important you document both, not just where you think your deficiencies lie. Make sure to date your entries so you can periodically scan through previous entries to see the progress you've shown over time. Take note if you see patterns or themes in your reflection and try to identify the root cause. This can be done by asking yourself *"why"* five times, to get at the core of an issue. This *'oldie but goodie'* method has been used for decades as part of Total Quality Management (TQM) according to the American Society for Quality (ASQ). That said, it's still highly effective for identifying the underlying issues for any challenge. Let's use an example to illustrate the method:

> *I noticed while self-reflecting that I always leave my Wednesday morning status meetings upset.*
> **Why is that?**
> *Well, it's because I never feel like I'm being heard.*
> **Why do you feel like you aren't being heard?**
> *Because Henry always interrupts me.*
> **Why does Henry always interrupt you?**
> *He says we only have time to discuss what's on the agenda, and my points aren't on the agenda.*
> **Why aren't your discussion points on the agenda?**
> *Because, I usually miss the deadline for submitting agenda talking points, which is due Monday at noon.*
> **Why do you miss the deadline?**
> *Well, after dropping the kids off at school, grabbing coffee with the team, catching up with my weekend emails, and submitting my weekly sales report, it's not always at the top of my to-do list.*
> **So, it sounds to me like it is a priority issue, not a collaboration issue?**

See how this basic method can help leaders get to the root causes of the mental challenges troubling them? Instead of blaming others, it's important to get at the core of the issue, which is often not at the surface layer.

Focus On Your Intentions, Your Actions, And Your Impacts

Beyond utilizing the root-cause technique, also focus your reflection on the **intention**, **action**, and **impact** of any situation you walk into as a leader. Focus on your behaviors and think about concrete examples of what you said or did. Write down what your intention was prior to the experience, the action (or behavior) you exhibited, and the impact of that action. Here is an example:

My intention: Deliver constructive feedback to a direct report during a performance review.

My action: I down-played the constructive points I wanted to make, focusing primarily on positive examples. When the time came to deliver areas for development, I sugarcoated my feedback by saying, *"But don't worry, everyone struggles with that. Just keep doing what you are doing, and you will be fine..."*

My impact: The direct report left the conversation without receiving the direct information they needed in order to develop into the best version of themselves.

Examining the ***intention, action***, and the ***impact*** of your experiences allows you to more clearly see gaps and blind spots in your leadership abilities. Using this model in your self-reflection will build greater awareness and alignment in what you set out to do *vs.* what you actually achieve.

Focus On What You Can Control

A common trap that leaders fall into when self-reflecting is spending time focusing on elements they can't control. It does little good spending time hashing out hypotheticals of what may or may not have been. If you find yourself doing this often, draw a clear line in your self-reflection entry by creating a table that delineates *In my control | Outside of my control*. Don't beat yourself up over things you cannot control, a far better use of your time will be to focus on what you *do* have the ability to change.

Share Your Self-Reflection

From time to time, open up and share some of your self-reflections with those you trust. This will be beneficial in multiple ways. First, it will show others that you take your own development seriously and are committed to continuous improvement. Secondly, their perspective on the same reflection can shed light on how accurate your self-awareness is with reality. If you desire to become a more development-focused leader, people will need to see your actions aligned with what you say. Sharing self-reflections can be a great way to practice what you preach, while also promoting a coaching culture within your teams. When sharing your reflections, make sure to choose people who will be honest with you, for better or worse.

Find The Balance

There is no one-size-fits-all approach to the amount of time you should or should not be devoting to self-reflection. You know yourself better than anyone. My guess is that you inherently know if you are carving out enough time to process your experiences in a meaningful way or if life is passing you by in a blur. Sometimes self-reflection is most powerful immediately after an experience, while in other instances it requires time and a serene place to fully introspect. Whatever is most helpful for you, strive for a balance. A good place to start may be placing 15 minutes on your calendar each week to check in with yourself. If you can't spare 15 minutes to reflect on your leadership ability, you're probably a person who needs 30.

The power of self-reflection is real. I have seen the eureka (a-ha moment) in hundreds of leaders as they discovered their own gaps through self-reflection. I will never forget a coaching conversation I had with a younger leader in a Fortune 100 technology company. She had risen through the ranks early in her career and was well respected at the highest levels of the organization. Her 'a-ha moment' occurred when she noticed—in group settings—her contributions were not often heard or acknowledged. She was a strong leader in one-on-one situations and had a gift for inspiring direct reports to hit their monthly goals; yet, in group settings, she felt like her voice was lost among her peers. During that vulnerable moment, she allowed herself to soak in that new realization, express some emotions, and think of ways she could work to improve that gap in her own leadership skill set.

Once leaders become honest with themselves, it's incredible to see the deep level of learning that can occur through the mental process of trying to understand their perception *vs.* their reality. Remember that self-reflection is not about beating yourself up—it's about discovering a greater understanding of your leadership ability. Always strive to find new ways to grow through self-reflection and you will find the buoyancy it provides in keeping your head above water.

Life Jacket #2: Self-Forgiveness

The ability to accept personal flaws and forgive oneself for mistakes.

> *"Forgiveness is the fragrance that the violet sheds on the heel that has crushed it."*
>
> - MARK TWAIN

One of the greatest challenges you will face in life is learning how to forgive. Whether you've thought about it or not, you have probably asked for forgiveness, and/or provided forgiveness to others, tens of thousands of times throughout your lifetime. You are not perfect; you will continue to screw up, make bad decisions, and regret actions that cause harm to others. Similarly, others are not perfect; they will screw up, hurt you, and ask for your forgiveness for their own shortcomings. While this concept is one we learn at a young age, it truly is a lifelong journey. It requires us to swallow our pride, let go of grudges, and move on for the benefit of all. Forgiveness provides a productive path forward when you allow it. However challenging it may be, forgiveness builds character, and strong character is needed for great leadership.

On the water, self-forgiveness is something every angler needs to learn. Whether it be a snag, a broken line, or piercing yourself with a hook, mistakes will happen. When you fish with sharp hooks (or take any chance in life), people can get hurt—including yourself. In a lot of ways, the responsibility of leadership can be thought of as how you handle sharp hooks. How do you care for them when casting your line? How do you protect yourself and others from getting hurt by them on your boat? How do you coach others when they now have sharp hooks at the ends of their lines? If used correctly, the hooks themselves will help you catch some of life's greatest lessons, but when neglected or used carelessly they can hurt yourself and others. Learning how to forgive (yourself and others) for unaccepted snags and lost lures along the way is part of leadership. When your conscience is clear, you will always be able to navigate yourself back to productive waters where you can fish and lead without resentment.

For this very reason, self-forgiveness is a crucial part of the *Release*. It is defined by a leader's ability to accept personal flaws and forgive personal mistakes. While forgiveness may not be a new topic for you, viewing it through the lens of leadership likely is. I suspect the reason self-forgiveness is not widely discussed in common leadership programs is because of its intimate nature. The process of self-forgiveness requires the ability for you to own up and address the personal battles that reside within you. Similar to self-reflection, self-forgiveness involves an ability to address the inner workings that underlie so many of the outward behaviors we display. Self-forgiveness is unique in that unlike other forms of forgiveness, it provides the stage for you to serve as both your own judge and defendant at the same time. Unfortunately, many leaders expect perfection of themselves, which leads them to play the role of a strict judge far more often than a sympathetic defendant.

Several years back, I had the opportunity to work with an executive coach who passed on some words of wisdom that still resonate with me to this day. We were discussing my results from a company-wide 360-degree feedback report when she realized that I had consistently rated myself much lower on a number of dimensions than my peers. She asked why I thought that was.

I responded, *"I think I am just really hard on myself, I tend to down-play my accomplishments and dwell on my mistakes."*

I continued by saying, *"I know that I shouldn't, but there is something ingrained in me that being hard on myself will make me better."*

She paused, and very deliberately said, *"Michael, I have a question for you... If one of your coworkers was 10 minutes late for a meeting would you forgive them or hold it against them?"*

I answered promptly, *"I would probably forgive them and try not to make a big deal of it."*

She nodded with a grin on her face, *"Now I'll ask you: how do you react toward yourself when you are 10 minutes late for a meeting?"*

I paused and let the question sink in. *"Truth be told,"* I said, *"I would probably beat myself up a bit, create a false narrative about how I'm always late, and assume that others were making negative judgments about my character."*

Saying those words out loud, the light bulb went off.

"Michael," she said, *"What if you started giving yourself the same slack you give others?"*

In that moment, I realized how unfairly I consistently judged myself compared to my peers. It became clear to me that my compassion for myself was drastically lower than the compassion I was willing to give to others. I owed myself a long-overdue apology for being so hard on myself all the time! Instead of judging myself with this heightened level of unfair scrutiny, I decided I would start practicing greater self-for-giveness and be kinder in the critical thoughts I held for myself.

As a leader, you can't afford to waste time or energy chastising yourself unfairly. Instead, allow yourself the same leeway you provide to others. One thing is certain—you will continue to fail—that's life. Learn from those failures and learn how to forgive yourself. The only person who will be by your side your whole life is you. Learn how to make peace with yourself and appreciate your own uniqueness.

The next time you recognize yourself being overly critical, take a deep breath and tell yourself you are forgiven. Say it out loud. If that means getting into your car, taking a walk, or standing in front of the mirror, do it until wherever it is you need to let go is released. This will feel awkward and seem pointless at first; however, it will help strengthen your ability to forgive yourself. You need to treat yourself just like you would any other person, so say the sincere phrase(s) out loud to make it real. It's a beautiful thing when you start becoming more comfortable in your own skin. Self-forgiveness provides you the opportunity to get out of your head and to start focusing on the impact you wish to create as a leader, and that sure beats playing the broken record of failures in your head over and over again.

Make Peace With Yourself

Early on in my career, I worked with a German colleague who loved telling a particular story whenever the topic of accepting developmental feedback came up during leadership workshops. He would recite the story the only way he knew how—with a smirk on his face and a thick German accent. Here is the paraphrased story from his perspective:

One time in Switzerland, I was facilitating the closing session of a leadership workshop. I noticed a man with an uneasy look on his face. The group of leaders had just completed three intense days of simulations, followed by receiving feedback on their leadership behaviors. A dialogue had begun among the group on how they were planning to incorporate the new information they received into their development planning.

When I called on the man with the confused look on his face to share what he learned he said, "I just don't know... I'm not sure how I am going to go back and tell my coworkers about my strengths and weaknesses. I'm not sure how they will take it, and it may make me look weak as a leader."

Before I had a chance to respond, an individual sitting next to the concerned man put his hand on his back and said, "My friend... I have news for you, your coworkers already know your weaknesses!" The room erupted in laughter—all being able to relate.

Blind spots, however difficult they may be to personally accept, are rarely hidden to those we interact with the most. Remember that others admire us for our flaws—it's what makes us uniquely awesome. Embracing them and continuously improving ourselves is what those around us want, not perfection.

 ## Life Jacket #3: Practicing Mindfulness
Prioritizing thoughts and actions that promote present awareness, gratitude, and inner peace.

In recent years, the topic of mindfulness has become increasingly popular. A basic search for mindfulness on Amazon will result in over 80,000 hits for books and other resources related to the topic. Beyond mainstream popularity, researchers are continuing to explore the impact mindfulness has on individual and organizational performance (Hyland, Lee, & Mills, 2015). While various studies over the years have shown positive mental and physical health benefits connected to mindfulness, more recent research is starting to examine the linkage between mindfulness and leadership effectiveness (Lippincott, 2018). While the appetite from both scientists and practitioners continues to grow, many leaders still struggle in finding the best way to incorporate mindfulness activities into their schedules in a consistent manner. For whatever reason, an uphill battle still seems to exist in convincing some leaders to dip their toes into the mindfulness pool. Some may be crippled by the perceptions of others, thinking they will be viewed as the *'crunchy granola'* type (which historically has not been well-received in corporate settings). Others may be open to practicing mindfulness, but have doubts in their own abilities to be any good at it because they have never really tried it. Some simply fail to follow through in a consistent manner, falling off the wagon before the cart has even moved. Regardless of what may have deterred you in the past, do yourself a favor and explore mindfulness again—without judgment from yourself or others.

A primary goal of practicing mindfulness is to increase your mind-body connection. This allows you to become more in tune with yourself, your environment, and the ebb and flow of your thoughts/emotions throughout the day. The mind-body connection is something that makes the human experience special and unique. As automation continues to revolutionize the workplace, leaders will need to accentuate their human side to enhance the value they can provide that robots cannot. Leaders with impeccable people skills, including the ability to promote mindfulness at work, will be more sought after than leaders with more tactical expertise that can be replaced through automation. Practicing mindfulness (and helping others do the same) will not only set you apart as a leader but also aid in combatting two of the most unhealthy byproducts leading in the digital age creates—stress and anxiety. As the digital world around us continues to rapidly accelerate, the lines between work and life will continue to blur. For this very reason, harnessing the benefits of mindfulness will become increasingly important—not only in your life but in those you lead.

Recall, from Chapter 2 that the human mind can process up to 60,000 conscious thoughts a day. If you are like me, you are probably starting to wonder how many of your own thoughts are productive, positive, and intentional? If human thoughts are largely repetitive, which research suggests, wouldn't it make more sense for leaders to fill their thoughts with gratitude, optimism, and self-love over thoughts of lack, pessimism, and self-doubt? In addition to thoughts, and perhaps even more fascinating, is the breathing activity humans demonstrate throughout a given day. The Cleveland Clinic posted baseline vital signs on its website in 2019. They indicated that the average person takes between 12-20 breaths per minute (Vital Signs, 2019). This translates to between 17,280 and 28,800 breaths a day. Even after subtracting 8 hours for sleep, we are still left with between 11,520 - 19,200 breaths each day. On a given day how many times do you consciously decide to take a deep breath in, and let it go? Less than five? Less than ten? Zero? Isn't it amazing how disconnected people have come from one of the most basic, yet vital tools we possess as humans, our breath?

There is no better time to start practicing mindfulness than right now. No more excuses, no more telling yourself you will start next month! Start now if you haven't already. Take a few extra diaphragm-filled breaths throughout your day or pick up a pen for five minutes to journal about what you are grateful for in a given moment. These small actions will have profound impacts over time if practiced regularly. Taking this first step may even open your mind to trying more advanced mindfulness activities, such as meditation or yoga down the road. Now, if joining a yoga studio doesn't sound like a good fit for you, don't force it. Instead, find other ways to unplug from distractions and focus your attention on the present moment. Try taking a walk in nature (or even just outside) without your cell phone. Try giving yourself ten minutes to do nothing but merely appreciate a beautiful sunset or sunrise. Increasing your present awareness will not only reduce stress and make you feel better, but it will also improve your ability to focus and listen to others without being distracted by a million thoughts. Before long, you will find yourself appreciating the small things in life, which will make a huge difference in your overall happiness and brain functionality.

As you start becoming more mindful, you will begin noticing others on the same wavelength. Energy feeds off of like-energy, and your vibe attracts your tribe. As you start practicing mindfulness, pay attention to the individuals who notice the positive changes practicing mindfulness yields for you. Don't be shy about sharing your experiences and encourage others to do the same. Keep in mind that you set the tone as a leader; others will follow your lead on the path to becoming more mindful.

G.R.I.N.

To help yourself and others on this wild journey of leadership development, I encourage you to learn how to *G.R.I.N.* Before going into this specific mindfulness method, I'm curious if you have ever heard someone say something to the effect of, *"I have no idea what that person's on, but I want some of that in my life!"* Whether or not you are the type of person who regularly finds themselves high on life or not, I want to share with you a simple, but effective, exercise I created to help you find more inner peace and happiness throughout the ups and downs of your life. Smile! You are about to learn how to *G.R.I.N.*

The *G.R.I.N.* is composed of 4 basic steps aimed to shift your mindset from one of worry and doubt to one of gratitude and confidence. It provides a new outlook on whatever situation you are dealing with. It takes less than 5 minutes to complete and only requires a pen, a piece of paper, and a willingness to feel better. It is crucial that you handwrite your responses, it will help you form stronger cognitive connections (Mueller & Oppenheimer, 2014). So, as old school as it sounds, find yourself a pen, piece of paper, and a good place to write down each element of the *G.R.I.N.*

At the top of your paper, write down the date and the acronym *G.R.I.N.* to serve as a reminder for each section you are about to fill out. The first three steps of the method are completed by writing down the phrases *"I am grateful…," "I release…,"* and *"I am…"* There is no limit to the number of responses required in each section; write as much as you need until you feel you have exhausted that section. For those of you who need guidelines, I personally try to write at least 3-5 responses for each of the first three sections. As you get the hang of this mindfulness exercise, you will begin documenting your responses in a more free-flowing fashion, which will likely result in several responses for each section.

With that, let's start with the first section. Write down all the things you are grateful for at the moment. As big or as little as they may be, just start writing some of the aspects of your life you are thankful for. Each time, write out the phrase *I am grateful* before your response. There is no judgment during this exercise, just be honest with yourself.

G.R.I.N.   **Date:**

I am **G**rateful _____

I am **G**rateful _____

I am **G**rateful _____

I am **G**rateful _____

I am **G**rateful _____

Once you have completed writing down all the things you are grateful for in the present moment, shift your attention to all the things you wish to release from your current consciousness. Think through all of the negative thoughts you tell yourself—all the thoughts that don't serve you and make you feel inadequate. What are the stories you tell yourself that hurt your self-esteem? It's time to let them go by writing down *"I release…"*

I **R**elease _____

I **R**elease _____

I **R**elease _____

I **R**elease _____

I **R**elease _____

As simple as this step is, calling out all of those limiting beliefs that have caused you pain over the years helps. Just because something has hurt you before, doesn't mean it needs to today. You are a stronger leader than any negative thought running around in your head—remind yourself of this especially when you are feeling down.

One of the best ways to build confidence and promote well-being is to write down *I am* statements. *I* and *am* are two of the strongest words in our vocabulary, yet many people use them so carelessly when speaking about themselves. Instead of using these words to put yourself down, reinforce the strengths you have through affirmations. Write down *"I am"* followed by an adjective, talent, or ability you bring to this world.

I am _____

I am _____

I am _____

I am _____

I am _____

After completing the first three sections of the *G.R.I.N.*, you shift your focus on what you want your new intention for the day to be. This is your chance, no matter what happened earlier that day, to create a blank slate, allowing you to write down the goal or intention that will help you take a positive step forward. No need to overwhelm yourself here, just write down one thing you want to move closer to today.

My New Intention is _____

The last step of the *G.R.I.N.* is to review what you wrote down—and smile. Yes, smile, and smile big while you're at it, because—whether you feel like it or not—a smile, either real or fake, can release chemical endorphins in your brain that lower stress and support your overall mood (Spector, 2017). To ensure I myself complete this final step I will sometimes write a self-assuring phrase like *"Michael, you got this ☺"* accompanied by a smiley face to finish the exercise on a high note. Once you've completed the *G.R.I.N.* it is important to recognize the fact that you just completed something few people do, and by doing so you have taken a proactive step to transform your mindset. Kudos to you.

To show you the beauty of this simple, yet effective exercise, I want to open up and share a time when I used the *G.R.I.N.* to move me out of a dark negative place. The following text is taken directly from my personal journal and is meant to illustrate the power of the *G.R.I.N.*

Context:

Today I woke up tired, worn out, and weary from the road. After working back-to-back-to-back 17-hour days with a cold, I'm so over this project. My wife was in a fender bender this morning, she is alright thank God, but I'm sure there will be repercussions with the insurance company I will have to deal with when I land this evening. Why is this happening to me? Does anyone else have to deal with problems like this? Do they work this hard and feel this exhausted? I can't deal with anything else right now. I am not in a good mental state... I need to change the story, I need to G.R.I.N.

G.R.I.N.   1-25-18

I am grateful to be going home on this plane right now
I am grateful that after this week of work I am taking vacation the entire next week
I am grateful that I have a safe and healthy wife in San Diego
I am grateful for my dog and the unconditional love he gives me
I am grateful to be alive

I release the need to blame others for my problems
I release the need to feel sorry for myself
I release the idea that no one else has it as hard as me
I release my ego telling me how unfair my life is

I am an intelligent man capable of dealing with adversity
I am kind and compassionate
I am able to forgive
I am able to bounce back stronger after being knocked down
I am who I am, and that's pretty awesome

My new intention is to use this example to help others find effective ways to deal with adversity and frustration in their lives.

You got this Michael, I believe in you ☺

Following this exercise, I went from a 2 (ready to lose it at any given moment) to a 7 (I'm OK and things will work out) on a 10-point happiness scale. I stopped blaming my problems on my job and co-workers. I stopped victimizing myself and began to breathe deeply, letting go of the petty stress I was feeling. I reminded myself that I am in control of how I feel and that no matter how bleak a situation looks or exhausted I feel, there is something to learn from it. I was able to transform an attitude that was weighing on me for hours upside down in 5 minutes. The *G.R.I.N.* has the power to save you from impulsive outbursts of anger. It can lower your stress and give you a new perspective regardless of the situation. It may even prevent you from saying something hurtful that could damage a professional or personal relationship. Practice it with consistency and begin to notice the positive changes that occur throughout your day.

Whatever your secret formula is to becoming more mindful, actively pursue it and follow through with an open mind. I never thought I would be the type of guy who writes in a journal and meditates, but it works for me. Find what works for you. You may be surprised how accepting people are of your efforts to become more mindful.

 ### Life Jacket #4 : Optimistic Mindset
Choosing to think and communicate in a way that promotes positivity.

The first fish I caught when I moved to California in 2016 was a grunion. I had never caught one before, truth be told, I didn't even know what a grunion was. To my surprise, I didn't use a pole, a hook, or even a net; I used my hands. I scooped the grunion up off the wet sand in Ocean Beach as it shimmered in the moonlight. It had been nearly a year since I had last caught a fish, and all I could do was smile. The months leading up to this moment included a move across the country, being onboarded to a new job, and getting plugged into a new community. Needless to say, fishing took a back seat to other life priorities for a little while. Eventually, though, it found me, like it always has—this time in the form of a *grunion run*. As I released the slippery little fish back into the Pacific Ocean that spring night, I couldn't help but acknowledge that my first fishing experience in California wasn't anything like I had ever imagined, but it was perfect nonetheless.

Letting go of expectations is key to experiencing sustained happiness. When you remove unrealistic expectations from the equation, you are able to find fulfillment in the smallest things. A dear friend of mine named Dennis once told me: *"Most people think that the key to happiness is having what you want, but the truth is happiness comes from wanting what you already have..."* Unfortunately, many people, leaders included, habitually crave to have more. They want the perfect job, perfect body, perfect bank account, perfect spouse, and—of course— perfect employees. Not only that, they want it all—right now. When perfection is the expectation, good enough is—well—not good enough. The game of setting unrealistic expectations leaves many leaders constantly filling a void instead of focusing on what they already have.

If Happiness Is What You Seek, Let Go Of Unrealistic Expectations

As I've mentioned throughout this book, online perceptions continue to distort realities serving as a catalyst to unhappiness in the digital age. Over time the mindless scrolling and comparisons can produce pessimistic thoughts that entertain ideas of lack over abundance. The grass will always appear greener on the other side, the fish will always look bigger in the picture, and someone will always have a faster, more shiny boat than you drive. The truth is, focusing on what you don't have will impair your ability to lead others. As a leader, you must ask yourself: *What mindset do I wish to instill in others? One of lack and negativity, or one of optimism and abundance?* Your mindset and subsequently actions are how you will be remembered as a leader, whether you realize it or not. The decision isn't that difficult—it's the awareness, discipline, and desire to see the world in a new way that trips most people up.

Working with an optimistic leader can profoundly impact team members trying to overcome their day-to-day challenges. When given the choice, which type of leader would you rather work for? One that promotes happiness over sadness, leads with encouragement over fear, and builds a culture that prioritizes progress over perfection? As I said, the decision is easy. More importantly, though, is to fully understand the part that you play in shaping the current environment you find yourself leading in. Organizational cultures are merely the reflection of employees' attitudes and beliefs. As a leader, your thoughts and actions contribute to your working environment much more than you probably realize. In need of a change, will you wait for the organization to make the first move, or will you initiate it? Honestly ask yourself right now if your day-to-day activities are part of the problem or part of the solution in your organization.

If you are a perfectionist (as a leader you very well could be) you probably have achieved a degree of success by raising your standards and sticking to your conventions. Your perfectionism, though, likely inhibits your happiness. When is anything ever good enough for the perfectionist?

The answer is never because they'll always find a nuance that could have been a little bit better, regardless of the overall accomplishment achieved. If perfectionist leaders can channel their efforts toward progress, not perfection, they will likely experience more optimistic thoughts. They will begin to appreciate successful growth on a more incremental and realistic level. Often in life, it is not the end result that makes people happy, but the ability to enjoy the ride along the way. If you only focus on the perfect end result, thoughts of inadequacy, doubt, and shame will fill your head along the way. Humans are not perfect, so why should our expectations of life reflect perfection? As a leader, learning how to channel progress as a building block toward future success will serve you far better than leading others through fear of perfection. While some leaders prefer to use fear-based leadership to drive short-term results, they often fail to recognize the negative trade-offs in terms of long-term commitment, cohesion, and sustainability that can be built with a more optimistic mindset. In today's work environment, younger generations will not tolerate working for tyrannical leaders possessing negative attitudes. They will pack up and leave poorly-led organizations for ones that more closely align with their values and working preferences. This does not imply that leaders should coddle team members or fabricate progress to keep everyone happy. Instead, they should set and coach to progress-based goals, rather than trying to fulfill a never-ending perfection gap. This is achieved by a leader's ability to reinforce realistic expectations, celebrate progress, and volunteer to be the change—instead of criticizing imperfections from an ivory tower.

I want to take a moment to share something with you on this topic that my mother taught me at a very young age. I hope her advice helps you when you are confronted with pessimism and negativity. She said, *"Michael, there will be times in your life that people will say or do hurtful things to you for no apparent reason. Remember that you never know what is going on in someone else's life; they may be hurting and simply taking their anger out on you. Don't take it personally, instead just smile and continue about your day in a positive way."* Through the years, I can't tell you how many times taking the high road my mother paved for me has allowed me to see negativity for what it really is.

Remember, that regardless of the situation, you as a leader always have the ability to change the narrative. Whether you tell yourself the glass is half-empty or half-full is a decision completely up to you. But know that the way you look at (and talk about) the water in the glass will impact your ability to lead. Creating a vision for a brighter tomorrow, regardless of current challenges, will better serve you, your team, and your mental well-being. Stop the downward spiral of negative thoughts before they begin. Trust that you are on the right path and that you are learning the lessons you need to learn on your journey.

Life Jacket #5 – Learning How to Unlearn

The ability to let go of previous thoughts, concepts, and opinions that no longer serve future goals.

At my last high school reunion, I remember striking up an interesting conversation with an old classmate of mine around the topic of unlearning. I asked her what she thought of the concept and if it should be taught in classrooms. Given that this was a few years ago and the topic was not yet widely popularized, I had to preface the discussion with what I meant by unlearning. As a side note, my classmate happened to be a teacher who had spent a lot of time educating others, which made the conversation that much more fascinating. I went on to describe that in school and in life we are taught countless lessons. From the time we are born, our development strongly depends on how quickly we can learn and retain new knowledge. Whether it's learning how to tie our shoes, recite the ABCs, or play a musical instrument, we spend a lot of time listening, applying, and being tested on all kinds of information. As a result, we end up creating strong neural connections between countless associations—some that continue to help us through life—and others that hold us back from exploring new growth. While I fully understand and support the importance of lifelong learning, I think it is just as important for people to learn how to unlearn concepts, ideas, or opinions that were previously instilled in them. My classmate looked at me, intrigued, but also slightly confused. After all, she probably wasn't planning on discussing metacognition (the brain thinking about the brain) at a class reunion. Regardless, I continued by explaining that many people hold onto rules, labels, or opinions that their parents and teachers have driven into them at earlier points in their lives. While many of the lessons we learned in school (e.g. reading, writing, and arithmetic) serve us throughout the course of our life, there are also some associations we need to unlearn—whether from childhood or adulthood—in order to fulfill the greatest version of ourselves.

An example of this a lot of people can relate to is the 'old food pyramid' that was taught to them in elementary school. Do you recall the guidelines recommended by public officials on how to maintain a healthy diet back in the 90s? It included 6-11 daily servings of bread, cereal, rice, and pasta as the base of the pyramid? Remember the dairy campaign that recommended three glasses of milk a day or the ongoing saga of whether or not eggs were good or bad for you? The point I am trying to make is that rules, or recommended guidelines, often change over time, requiring people to have to unlearn what was once considered *truth*. This process requires tremendous effort and a willingness to openly challenge previous mental connections people may have made. In order to unlearn concepts previously ingrained in you, you must stop feeding the old connections in your brain and start creating new ones that better serve your ability to lead.

Unlearning Creates Space For New Learning

The idea of unlearning doesn't only apply to lessons you have learned, it also applies to feedback, or labels others may have given you at a previous time in your life. As a child in second grade, I remember being placed in the *red* reading group. The *red* group was the group dedicated to students with mid-level reading ability, the *green* group was for students with the highest reading ability, and the *blue* group was for the students with the lowest reading ability. Of course, the teacher didn't tell us this point-blank, but we all knew it. The mere fact that I still remember this today shows you the profound impact it had on me. What really triggered me at that young age was when a student from first grade was moved up and placed in the *green* group over me, a second grader! I took it personally, not being in the *green* group. I started allowing that label to dictate my behavior, I started not enjoying reading class, and resented going to the library with the other kids. I began to believe that I was a bad reader and that I always would be. Over the years, I have worked hard to unlearn this limiting belief. The truth is, I actually really enjoy reading, but may have never arrived at this conclusion if I hadn't stopped reinforcing the negative label I created for myself at such a young age. I had to release the pain I felt as a second-grader in order to transform into a better version of myself today—a reader. Having not done so would have likely inhibited my drive to write this book, let alone enjoy reading the works of others.

Looping back to the conversation with my classmate; I could tell she was beginning to understand what I meant by the concept of unlearning. She posed two really good questions: *"How would you teach students to 'unlearn' and how would you measure it?"* I said, *"Excellent questions, I have some ideas, but don't want to talk your ear off all night about it."* She smiled and we both went our separate ways, catching up with old friends we hadn't seen since the days of the old food pyramid.

As creatures of habit, unlearning is difficult. It is much easier for us to continue prescribing to a previously learned concept then releasing it for a new one. Given the disruption and speed of modern-day life, leaders will need to build the skill of unlearning to stay agile.

Throughout your leadership journey, you will learn a lot of concepts and you will receive a lot of feedback. Remember to stay malleable—no one piece of advice or feedback should define the type of leader you are throughout your entire life. Soak in the meaningful lessons provided to you and release the lessons that limit the best version of yourself.

Build a leadership muscle that allows you to go with the flow, by being able to both learn and unlearn.

I leave you with two nuggets of wisdom by the late Dr. Wayne Dyer that have served me well through my own *Release*. The first is a saying I have found useful when I feel myself resisting new information or ideas that may not be aligned with my expectations. *"Have a mind that is open to everything and attached to nothing"* (Dyer, 2010). If you are truly able to let go and listen, new ideas or thoughts will be seen as opportunities, not triggers. The second is a powerful metaphor I stumbled upon one night watching YouTube clips of Wayne. It was taken from a seminar he was teaching to help people move on from past transgressions. In the clip, Wayne credited the philosopher Alan Watts for this imagery, but Wayne himself made it popular in the self-help community. He said, and I paraphrase, that your life is like a boat. Imagine you are heading up a river at 40mph. As you look behind you, you see the wake that is left behind from the motor propelling the boat. Today, you stand in the middle of the boat and can choose how fast or slow you want to drive and which way you would like to steer it into the future. The wake is simply the trail of previous life experiences that serve to remind us where we came from—nothing more—nothing less. The challenge many people have is acknowledging that the wake doesn't propel the boat forward. That is: no excuse, victimization, or past pain will ever be able to propel the boat the same way positive energy in the present moment can. You get to decide right here and now the speed, trajectory, and direction you wish to steer your boat (Dyer, 2016). Release whatever it is from your wake that holds you back, your present momentum depends on it.

CHAPTER 7

Conclusion

After the *C.A.T.C.H.* & *Release*

"The charm of fishing is that it is the pursuit of what is elusive, but attainable, a perpetual series of occasions for hope."

-JOHN BUCHAN

Many years have passed since that unforgettable day on Lake St. Clair, but the lesson I caught is timeless. *You can either let the events in your life define you, or you can define the events in your life.* Sometimes you have to lose a fish in order to catch something more meaningful. The anguish, doubt, and shame I felt that day and subsequent years to follow may seem trivial to some, but I know that it was all necessary for my own growth. I needed to feel the pain of failure in order to transform it into something more powerful. I needed to learn how to release a young man's ego in order to change the story into something that could help others. When I look back at the picture of Bob and me holding up his three fish, I now see a great bond created on the water that day. Fishing with Bob during practice and the day of the tournament itself forged an everlasting friendship. While Bob may have contributed more to our overall results on paper, I still played an important supporting role. I spent several hours that weekend strategizing with the team, reviewing lake maps, and preparing equipment, not to mention netting Bob's fish. It took me some time, but I finally realized that leadership comes in all shapes and sizes. It's not always about the end result, but rather *the journey along the way.* Even though another fish could have helped us place higher, losing it has provided me with so much more substance in the long-run. My hope is that by sharing this story with you, you are able to recognize whatever disappointment, shame, or guilt still lingers in your heart. All leaders have a story of *the one that got away*, but not all leaders allow themselves to discover the deeper lessons from their plight. In the end, a leader's happiness and effectiveness boils down to their ability to *C.A.T.C.H. & Release* both the seen and unseen elements in their life.

As for Bob, he never stopped chasing his dream which came true on September 14th, 2019 when he won the Bassmaster Central Open at Grand Lake qualifying him to fish in the 50th Annual Bassmaster Classic in 2020.

The picture snaps, the memory is made, and the *C.A.T.C.H.* is *Released*. Reflecting back on your leadership experiences, all the lessons you've learned, the lives you've impacted, and progress you've made, you can't help but notice that the ending is somewhat different than you imagined. The truth is our realities rarely match our original expectations. Some experiences exceed them, others disappoint, and some leave us completely puzzled. There are many culprits that contribute to the disconnect—having unrealistic goals from the onset, inaccurately predicting how certain events will make us feel over time—and a general lack of gratitude in life. Regardless of which pitfall is at play at any given moment, people are often at a loss trying to make sense of their emotions when one chapter in their life closes and another begins.

Leading through the *C.A.T.C.H. & Release* will not immunize you from experiencing the full spectrum of emotions associated with leadership. In fact, the opposite should hold true if you are following the model accordingly. You should be experiencing levels of discomfort at various times during your leadership journey. How you respond to the growing pains of leadership is ultimately what will cement your legacy. Throughout your journey, there will be times you feel exhilarated by your accomplishments—the person you have become, the new knowledge you have gained, and the people you have positively influenced. At other times, you will feel nostalgic and perhaps even saddened to come to terms with the fact that you can't turn back the clock and relive some of your greatest milestones and memories. No catch, whether your own or someone else's, can ever be fully replicated. It can only be experienced in the now. As you process all of these experiences and emotions resulting from the completion of a *C.A.T.C.H. & Release,* you may wonder, *"What's next?"* That's the million-dollar question every leader seeking to solidify their legacy finds themselves asking at one point or another. How do you take the next step forward when you finally feel confident leading from the ground you stand on? The answer doesn't reside in some cosmic time machine, nor in digging your feet deeper into the sand. With or without you, the journey continues as future leaders come to age and explore new ways to lead themselves.

At all costs, resist the urge to rest on your laurels—no matter how great you think they may be. Doing so only deprives yourself (and others) from the growth needed to self-actualize. Every day, just like every cast, has a way of presenting new opportunities to succeed. When you start becoming more in tune with your environment and truly demonstrate a growth mindset, you will discover the unique answer to your million-dollar question. While your next cast may differ from the leader standing next to you, the starting place will always be the same.

New growth begins with the acknowledgment that a leader cannot continue fishing the same waters, with the same anglers, catching the same fish, and expect the same fulfillment. As a leader, you must continue to challenge yourself and fight the false sense of security the status quo provides. You must learn to not only embrace the unknown—but begin to crave it. No matter how heavy your feet feel in the sand, you must make an effort to take the next step forward. Your greatest impact has always depended—and will continue to depend—on your ability to fight fear while venturing to places unknown.

Learning how to build a healthy relationship with fear will lead you to unimaginable places. Your greatest triumphs, the number of lives you impact, and the strength of your legacy all hinge on your ability to conquer the unknown. Doing so will not only help you grow but it will encourage others to do the same. Your ripple has the potential to be felt all over the world, so jump into your fear and make a splash.

Establish A Healthy Relationship With Fear

Overcoming fear is easier said than done. To be successful, you must first undergo a paradigm shift where you begin to see fear for what it really is—a precursor to meaningful growth. No matter how dark, intimidating, or cold the new waters you seek to navigate may be, you always hold the power to course-correct your ship. Instead of allowing fear to flood your mind with negative thoughts and anxiety, listen to what it is trying to tell you. Let fear guide your self-discovery in answering your million-dollar question. If the new waters you seek to explore don't produce some level of fear, you are looking in the wrong direction. Challenge yourself by asking what it is you are exactly afraid of. Are these thoughts warranted or fabrications of a myth you have been telling yourself for quite some time now? Steering your boat in an unfamiliar direction, just like taking that next step forward, comes with risk, but also great reward. When doubt creeps in, remind yourself that every meaningful accomplishment in your life began with some degree of uncertainty—so naturally—your next leadership move should too. Fear is nothing more than the shadow of opportunity. At first glance, the shadow can frighten you, but when brought into the light for what it really is, it provides you a path forward to grow into a stronger and wiser leader.

It's important to acknowledge that there is a flip side to fear that also needs to be addressed. Fear serves as a powerful mechanism to protect humans from danger. Unfortunately, it's not always easy to know when fear is truly protecting people from harm and when it is just clouding the ability to navigate uncharted waters. A key to your leadership effectiveness depends on your ability to learn how to recognize when fear is inhibiting your growth and when it is trying to save you from danger. There will be times when some waters are too dangerous for even the best leaders to tread. Some risks are simply not worth the reward, and fear can serve to save leaders from catastrophic decisions.

To determine which kind of fear you are dealing with, first, ask yourself if the next steps you are considering are life-threatening. Sometimes, we think of leadership decisions as life and death, when, in reality, they simply are not. Last time I checked, no one has died from having to present to a board, make a difficult budget decision, or even fire someone, yet some leaders will work themselves up to make it appear that way. The key point is to learn how to understand your fear more rationally. Don't be a leader who gets worked up over everything, doing so will only cloud your ability to grow.

To know the level of fear you are dealing with and the legitimacy of your concerns, I encourage you to communicate your fear(s) with someone you trust. The individual must possess the ability to be both empathetic and candid with you. That balance is key in helping you sort out the severity of your fear. All alone, fear has a way of expanding irrationally like a balloon ready to burst; however, when fear is communicated to another, the pressure almost always seems to be relieved, if not deflated completely. Never feel alone when dealing with fear, know that all leaders face fear. If you are anxious about something, there is a good chance some other leader has also felt anxious about the same exact thing. So, be a leader and seek counsel when you feel fear mounting. In doing so, you will limit the toll that paralyzing thoughts and actions can have on your ability to lead. Sometimes, all it takes is an outside perspective to reground you when the volume of your fears are amplified. As you continue to develop yourself, insecurities will continue to surface. A balanced perspective will be key in mitigating the harmful effects excessive fear can have on your mind.

In your efforts to establish a better relationship with fear, avoid complacency by all means necessary. Complacency—not fear—is the greatest inhibitor to growth. A certain level of fear is actually vital to the growth process. My father-in-law once told me that nervous fears, or butterflies, serve to validate that you are about to do something great. He would say, *"Nerves are just preparing your body to do something it has never done before."* The next time you find yourself getting nervous, remember his words of wisdom, they have served me well over the years.

When taking on new leadership responsibilities, it may feel like you are starting over, or even taking a step backward. Trust in yourself that you are not. You are exactly where you need to be on the journey, one step closer to expanding the positive impact you can have on this earth. You have the tools, knowledge, and resources needed to succeed. Instead of reinventing the wheel, let the *C.A.T.C.H. & Release* Model continue to guide you as you push yourself to overcome the new challenges you face in your role.

Leadership development is a cyclical process. Each phase begins the same way as it ends—with a level of uncertainty, a new challenge, and an opportunity to better yourself. Regardless of where you are on your leadership journey, strengthening your skills, interacting with diverse individuals, setting others up for success, and finding healthy ways to *Release* will continue to be paramount to your success. Whether you lead a team of 1 or a team of 10,000 the model still works the same. The *C.A.T.C.H. & Release* Model was designed to serve as an aid to help you when you feel unfulfilled or paralyzed at any given moment. While the boat, crew, and size of fish you seek may grow, the steps within the *C.A.T.C.H. & Release* will always provide a path forward. The dock will always serve to ground you and provide a safe environment as you continue to learn new ways to *Cast Your Line*. The new casting techniques you develop will not only serve you but also will aid in your ability to *Attract Diverse Anglers*. You can count on your patience being tested, especially when you fish new waters, but keep in mind that your legacy will be carried on when you decide to *Tie Their Knot*. The overall impact of your legacy will largely be determined by how well you individually *Coach Their Cast*. As fish begin to get caught with more regularity and in larger sizes, your efforts to *Honor Their Catch* will not go unnoticed. Continue to celebrate the successes of others while also finding healthy ways to *Release* your own limiting beliefs that inhibit your potential.

Throughout it all, stay nimble, stay hungry, and know that the dock will always be there waiting for you to *F.I.S.H.*, *S.N.A.G.*, and *G.R.I.N.* as you start the process all over again.

LEGACY OF LEADERSHIP FRAMEWORK

In closing, I leave you with a diagram to help center you in your efforts to establish a legacy of leadership. There are three major components to the diagram below: *Achieving Results*, *Developing Others*, and *Developing Yourself.*

When the winds of leadership push and pull your sails into different directions, your job will be to anchor yourself in the middle of these three major components. Note that effective leadership is not synonymous with any one or two of these areas. The strongest leadership legacies are built by the collective power of all three.

Having had a chance to review the diagram, take a moment to ask yourself which of the three main circles you currently find yourself operating from the most. Is there one particular circle you are naturally drawn to? Which circles are 2nd and 3rd, respectively? Which are natural strengths and which are natural development areas for you? Do you find yourself primarily operating from one, two, or an equal balance of all three?

Establishing a lasting legacy of leadership without incorporating all three components into your leadership practice is nearly impossible. This is because great leaders do not only achieve results, nor do they solely focus on the development of themselves or others. In fact, excelling in two of these areas at the same time, even though it may commonly be mistaken for, is not great leadership. If you ever find yourself feeling stagnant or ineffective in your ability to lead, it is likely the result of being stuck in what I refer to as one of the *Comfort Zones of Leadership*. Each comfort zone can give a leader a false sense of overall effectiveness. To better understand these comfort zones and some of the pros and cons associated with each, examine the tables below.

COMFORT ZONES OF LEADERSHIP

Zone of Autonomy

An individual who operates with a high degree of independence, prioritizing personal results and self-development, while largely neglecting the development of others.

Pros	Cons
You don't need to rely on others for success	You limit your leadership reach and impact
You are the sole decision-maker	You miss opportunities to learn from others
You personally receive recognition for achievements	You fail to provide coaching and feedback regularly

Zone of Dependence

An individual who operates with a high degree of dependencies, prioritizing team results and the development of others, while largely neglecting self-development.

Pros	Cons
You can delegate tasks to others	You depend on others in order to achieve results
You can learn new skills and knowledge from those around you	You neglect opportunities for personal development
You can accomplish more and share in collective successes	You do not thrive in an autonomous environment

Zone of Development - An individual who primarily focuses on the development of themselves and others, while failing to achieve tangible results.

Pros	Cons
You are intrinsically rewarded by the activities that support development in yourself and others	You often fail at delivering the kind of tangible results (e.g. sales goals, operational KPIs, etc.) others can easily measure
You build trusting relationships focused on growth and continuous improvement	You risk being judged by others as merely a "soft skills" leader
You share and receive developmental wisdom	You may miss opportunities to receive recognition given the confidentiality of your work

Being an effective leader requires you to acknowledge your own leadership comfort zone. By doing so, you can identify where a better balance exists and how to channel your development efforts. Throughout your career, you must continually seek to achieve results, develop others, and develop yourself. Striving for this balance will take a tremendous amount of effort, but it will result in you being a more effective and sustainable leader. Keep in mind that your leadership journey will continue to evolve as you grow and take on new challenges. Allow this framework to serve as a compass to help you better understand how you spend your time and energy. As an ongoing exercise, I encourage you to periodically draw this Venn diagram and reflect where you think you are operating from at any given moment. Does a greater balance exist for you and the way you want to be remembered as a leader?

You may be curious how the leadership concepts and lessons I laid out in the *C.A.T.C.H. & Release* Model align with this framework. Think of the *Legacy of Leadership Framework* as the *"what"* and the *C.A.T.C.H. & Release* Model as the *"how."* A legacy is what you are trying to be remembered by long after your career. The *C.A.T.C.H. & Release* Model provides the steps you can take now to keep you centered and balanced throughout your journey. Equally, if not more important, than the *"what"* and the *"how,"* is your *"why."* Don't be a leader just to lead, be a leader who inspires impact through your *"why."* If you haven't done so yet, I encourage you to revisit and complete your Leadership Statement from the introduction to help you document your *"why."* Similarly, make sure to take the *C.A.T.C.H. & Release* Leadership Index (CARLI) at www.catchingleadership.com if you haven't yet. If you have, now may be a good time to reexamine your results.

Versatility is the real strength of the *C.A.T.C.H. & Release* Model. It can be used holistically or piecemeal to realign and center leaders at any given time. If you are either new to leadership or seeking to train aspiring leaders, you may be inclined to spend time addressing each dimension, starting with *Cast Your Line*. If you are a seasoned leader and have a good grasp of what your leadership gaps are, you may be inclined to hone in on one or two constructs within a dimension to round out your leadership ability. My intention from the start was to create a model to help all leaders seeking to cast a lasting legacy regardless of their unique experiences and background. Seen below are how the six dimensions of the *C.A.T.C.H. & Release* Model align with the *Legacy of Leadership Framework*.

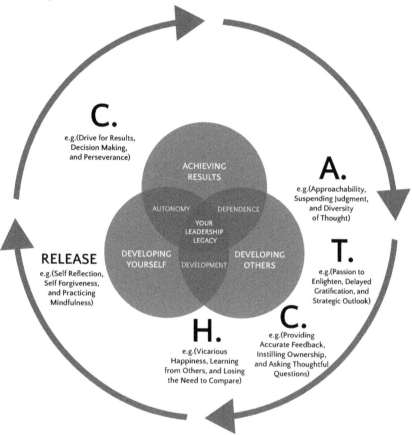

As humans, there is unfinished work within us all. While the *C.A.T.C.H. & Release* Model can be an excellent resource to guide your leadership development, the work has always been, and will always be up to you. The words in this book are just that—words. The magic begins when the words are brought to life through your actions. Be the leader who others don't just admire, but carry on your legacy within their own leadership practice.

As this book comes to an end, a new chapter begins. One where you are now the author, captain, and storyteller. Be kind to yourself as you continue to fight the good fight. Strive for progress over perfection and let go of whatever pain still haunts you! Discover whatever it is that deeply motivates you inside and take a giant leap forward knowing that you have caught something few ever find! Tight Lines!

Appendix

It's not every day you stumble across a storefront offering to dish out some of its most valuable secrets. What if the secrets were free, well-intended, and only required one ask of you: pay them forward? Would you be willing to listen with an open mind or would you walk by in pure skepticism? If you did decide to listen and you received some new knowledge, would you openly share it, or be tempted to keep it to yourself? As you contemplate what you think you would do, I feel compelled to share some of mine.

MY FISHING SECRETS

Fishing Secret #1: Fish bite the best when the wind is from the West. Consequently, they bite the least when the wind is from the East. The natural flow of the jet stream follows a west to east pattern, which is natural to a fish's environment. When the wind comes from the east, it's typically the result of an unusual front or storm that can cause fish to be more finicky until the abnormal weather pattern subsides.

Fishing Secret #2: Black is the color to use when water and skies are in dark hues. In stained water on a cloudy day throw a darker lure. On a clear and bright day throw a lighter-colored lure. Always put yourself in the environment of the fish. If visibility is low in stained water with overcast skies, fish are most likely seeing a silhouette of their prey. Unable to pick up on unique colors, it is more important to give fish a dark object to strike. The opposite holds true when visibility is high. In these instances, you want to use more realistic lures that mimic baitfish. White happens to be one of the most universal fishing colors because most fish have shades of white on their undersides.

Fishing Secret #3: The bird's the word. Fish in areas where you see large birds residing. If you come across a blue herring or bald eagle hanging out close to the water, there is usually a good reason for it. Large birds forage on baitfish, and wherever there are baitfish there are game fish.

Fishing Secret #4: Keep the radio low if you don't want the day to be slow. Every time you come across a new fishing spot, whether onshore or in your boat, being as stealthy as possible is a huge advantage! Avoid making unnecessary noise or commotion if you want to capture the element of surprise.

Fishing Secret #5: What's on your hands can impact the fish you land. Often overlooked by anglers are the smells and substances that reside on their hands when they handle their lures. If you smoke or chew tobacco and don't wash your hands before touching your lure you very well could be inhibiting your success. The same can be said with microfibers or other materials like carpet or clothing that stick to your lures. A fish examining your lure up close will think twice if a foreign odor or material is detected.

Fishing Secret #6: Look at every fish you hook! Take note of the size, color, and what they have been eating. Notice if anything can be seen inside their mouths. Gently squeeze their stomach to determine if they have been eating baitfish (smooth) vs. crayfish (rocky). The belly and mouth can provide great insight into what a fish has been recently foraging on. To the best of your ability, try to match the hatch by mimicking the fish's prey with what's in your tackle box. The overall color of the fish can also give you clues about the oxygen levels in the water. The paler the fish (relative to the natural color of its species) could indicate less oxygen in its blood. If that's the case the fish may have less energy resulting in you having to slow down your presentation to be more effective.

Fishing Secret #7: Never wipe the protective slime off a fish you plan to release. Removing this protective coating hurts the fish and makes you look like an uneducated angler. Use your towel to dry your hands, not the fish.

Fishing Secret #8: The GREATEST BASS LURE OF ALL TIME is Reaction Innovations' Sweet Beaver. The best color is California 420 (watermelon with red fleck). Ok, I can't lie... the same lure in black and blue can be good too. No bias here whatsoever ☺...

Secrets—every angler has them—but not every angler shares them. These coveted tidbits of knowledge, on the best spots, lures, and techniques have the ability to impact success exponentially. Secrets, though, must always be taken with a grain of salt because what works one day for one angler may not work another day for another angler. In fishing, or leadership for that matter, there are no absolutes—well maybe just one. If you never try (*Cast Your Line*), you'll never catch leadership. All other tips are not guaranteed, just information that may or may not help you on your journey. Regardless of what your fishing or leadership secrets are, I encourage you to share them with others. Pay forward helpful knowledge whenever you can. This process is mutually beneficial for you and others hungry to learn. Hoard knowledge and knowledge will be hoarded from you—enlighten others and you yourself will be enlightened!

In life, when does knowledge become a secret? Is it the moment you realize that you know something that few others do? Does it require one, two, or ten successful outcomes (e.g. one bite *vs.* several bites in a row) before a hunch becomes a valued secret? How long is a secret good for? Is there danger in passing on secrets that have helped you with others? Which is worse, a person who abuses secrets shared with them, or a person who never shares their secrets at all?

Unlike some anglers who wish to hoard their secrets to themselves, leaders should be willing to openly share their knowledge of success with others. When asked to open up their tackle box and let others peek inside, they should not be threatened or scared. In being transparent, the leader may spark new ideas and encourage others to expand their own repertoire of lures and casting techniques. A confident leader knows that sharing their path to success doesn't limit their future success, in fact, it only strengthens it.

With all this talk of secrets, I would like to share some leadership secrets I gleaned from the *C.A.T.C.H. & Release* Leadership Index (CARLI) Pilot. If you haven't yet taken the instrument and wish to do so, visit www.catchingleadership.com to learn more.

CARLI PILOT BACKGROUND

The *C.A.T.C.H. & Release* Leadership Index (CARLI) is a psychometric tool used to measure leadership ability across the six dimensions of the *C.A.T.C.H. & Release* Model. Each dimension contains a subset of the 34 leadership constructs discussed throughout the book. At its core, the focus of the instrument is centered around leadership development. It was never intended nor designed to be used for hiring, firing, or promotion decisions; but rather, a new way to help individuals and groups explore their own leadership through the lens of the *C.A.T.C.H. & Release* Model. During the pilot, the instrument was administered to 115 leaders averaging 13.3 years of leadership experience. The table below breaks down the demographic information related to the leaders who participated in the pilot.

Pilot Participant Profile (n = 115)

Leadership Status	
Currently serving in a leadership role	83.5%
Previously served in a leadership role	16.5%
Leadership Experience	
Average number of years formally serving in a leadership role	13.3 years
Median number of years formally serving in a leadership role	10 years
Number of Direct Reports	
1-5 people	37.4%
6-10 people	27.8%
11-25 people	16.5%

26-50 people	6.1%
50+ people	10.4%
N/A	1.7%
Gender	
Male	57.4%
Female	42.6%
Generational Split and Age at Time of the Pilot (2018)	
Millennial (Born between 1977-1995)*	23-41 years old	49.6%
Generation X (Born between 1965-1976)*	42-53 years old	21.7%
Baby Boomer (Born between 1946-1964)*	54-72 years old	27.8%
Traditionalists (1945 and before)*	73+ years old	0.9%
Generations defined by The Center for Generational Kinetics, 2018	

Industry Split	
Construction	2.6%
Educational Services	14.8%
Government	3.5%
Healthcare	13.0%
Manufacturing	5.2%

Professional / Business Services	38.3%
Other (e.g. Technology, Insurance, Retail, etc.)	22.6%

The way you should interpret the results of the CARLI Pilot is similar to the way you should interpret landing your first fish at a new lake. Does the initial catch tell you everything you need to know about the new body of water you are fishing? Of course not. Should the specific lure, location, and time of day of your catch dictate how you approach the lake in the future? Well, yes and no. Yes, you should leverage the new information gleaned from your catch, but no because the sample size is small and there is still much to be learned. The findings or *"secrets"* I share with you from the CARLI should be treated the same way. While some interesting findings were discovered, my intention is to continue to fish for more data and run additional analyses in the future. This will allow me to learn even more about the large body of water that is leadership. Use the knowledge I am about to share to your benefit, but don't necessarily treat it as gospel until you go out and cast your own line. In the meantime, here is my fishing report to date. I hope it helps you catch something meaningful in the meantime.

MY LEADERSHIP SECRETS

CARLI Secret #1: Communication is KING! When asked what the most important skill for leaders to learn, the most common open-ended responses from piloted leaders were communication and listening. This finding reminds me of a video I saw online where Warren Buffett shared that honing one's communication skills (both written and verbal) was one of the best ways aspiring leaders could invest in themselves. This advice serves as a great reminder for all of us to remember that improving our communication skills is a lifelong process.

CARLI Secret #2: The three most common answers leaders gave when asked what skill was most difficult to learn were: *Communication*, *Emotional Intelligence*, and *Inspiring/Motivating Others*. All three of these skills require a tremendous amount of emotional and social awareness. An effective leader doesn't simply make demands, they must fully understand their audience and find the appropriate ways to engage them. Each of these three constructs is defined in Chapter 1: *Cast Your Line*, which I consider to be foundational for effective leadership. This finding highlights the importance for all leaders to continually go back to the dock to revisit the fundamentals of leadership periodically.

CARLI Secret #3: 24.3% of surveyed leaders indicated that the *most important skill* for a leader to learn was also the *most difficult* for them to learn. The fact that nearly 1 in 4 surveyed leaders offered parallel responses for these two open-ended questions suggests to me that a fair number of leaders understand that what is most worthwhile to develop is often the most challenging. Aspiring leaders could interpret this finding as support for the old adage "*swallow the frog,*" in your leadership practice. Try tackling the most difficult development areas first, which will pay greater dividends down the road for you. This idea parallels with the concept of self-control which is captured in the leadership construct *Delayed Gratification* from Chapter 3: *Tie Their Knot*.

CARLI Secret #4: Average scores for the *Release* were lower than any other dimension within the *C.A.T.C.H. & Release* Model. This finding supports the idea that leaders today may not be prioritizing efforts to let go of unhealthy thoughts and fully unplug from distractions. As the world becomes more digitized, it will be crucial for leaders to find better ways to *Release* in order to promote longevity, prevent burnout, and establish optimal mental health. I believe the *Release* will only continue to grow in importance over time, so start developing these skills now to better position yourself to be the most effective leader you can be in the future.

CARLI Secret #5: The 12 collective constructs making up *Cast Your Line* were rated the highest among piloted leaders. Given that the constructs defined in *Cast Your Line* are foundational to effective leadership, it is of little surprise that surveyed leaders responded to these items with their highest self-reported scores. This finding supports the idea that the subsequent dimensions in the *C.A.T.C.H. & Release* Model may offer greater learning opportunities for more experienced leaders.

What has been shared with you is the CARLI fishing report (for now), but rest assured there will be more to come. In the meantime, I need to head back to the dock to relearn how to cast my own line. I've decided that there is still much for me to learn in the world of leadership and fishing. To expand my own horizons, I have decided to take up fly fishing, a casting technique I know little about. I honor this opportunity and look forward to developing in a completely new way. One cast, snag, and tangled line at a time I will be catching leadership and invite you to do the same.

C.A.T.C.H. & Release® Leadership Index Glossary

Chapter 1: Cast Your Line - *Understand Your Skill Set and Lead by Example*

Adaptability – The ability to quickly modify behavior to meet changing needs.

Emotional Intelligence – The ability to accurately interpret, regulate, empathize, and respond to the emotions in oneself and others.

Authenticity – Behaving in a way that is genuine with one's own natural tendencies.

Continuous Improvement – The mindset that one can continually learn and develop to create a better version of themselves.

Perseverance – The unwavering strength and determination to achieve goals despite challenges and setbacks.

Inspirational Influence – The ability to influence others by connecting personal experiences to emotions resulting in an increased commitment to act.

Clear Communication – The ability to communicate in a transparent and concise manner; being able to simplify complex concepts into language easily understood by others.

Courage – Displaying the strength to act during situations of uncertainty, especially when others refuse to act.

Decision Making – The ability to thoughtfully process information in a timely manner and accept responsibility for the outcomes of one's decisions.

Integrity – Behaving in alignment with high moral standards; doing the "right" thing regardless of the circumstance.

Drive for Results – The proactive pursuit to accomplish tasks and achieve results.

Effective Delegation – The ability to assign appropriate tasks to individuals in a way that promotes development and accountability through the trust that others will carry out tasks effectively.

Chapter 2: Attract Diverse Anglers - *Diversify Your Network and Challenge Your Understanding of the World*

Approachability – Behaving in a way that welcomes interactions with others.

Suspending Judgment – The ability to suspend initial judgment.

Inclusiveness – Providing equal opportunities for all to participate.

Curiosity – An ongoing desire to acquire new knowledge.

Diversity of Thought – Proactively seeking out new ideas and perspectives to improve one's overall understanding.

Chapter 3: Tie Their Knot - *Set Aside Personal Ambition for Mutual Long-Term Success*

Strategic Outlook – The ability to keep a long-term strategy in mind during day-to-day activities.

Delayed Gratification – The ability to postpone immediate rewards in exchange for greater long-term rewards.

Passion to Enlighten – Experiencing a great sense of fulfillment when educating others.

Chapter 4: Coach Their Cast - *Deliver Ongoing Feedback and Encouragement to Help Emerging Leaders Develop Their Own Skill Sets*

Deliberate Mindset – The ability to refrain from impulsive thoughts and actions.

Providing Accurate Feedback – The ability to constructively communicate strengths and development areas in others using behavioral examples.

Instilling Ownership – Building accountability in others to follow through on their commitments.

Asking Thoughtful Questions – The ability to ask open-ended questions in a way that allows others to draw meaningful conclusions.

Discovering Learning Opportunities Unconditionally – The ability to find meaningful lessons regardless of the situation.

Chapter 5: Honor Their Catch - *Celebrate and Find Fulfillment in the Successes of Others*

Vicarious Happiness – Experiencing positive emotions through the happiness and success of others.

Humility – Displaying modesty and humbleness.

Losing the Need to Compare – Avoiding the need to measure personal success against the successes of others.

Learning from Others – The ability to apply lessons learned from others to one's own life.

Chapter 6: *Release* - *Self-Reflect, Let Go, and Show Gratitude for What Matters Most*

Self-Reflection – Prioritizing time to think about one's own thoughts, behaviors, and impact.

Self-Forgiveness – The ability to accept personal flaws and forgive oneself for mistakes.

Practicing Mindfulness – Prioritizing thoughts and actions that promote present awareness, gratitude, and inner peace.

Optimistic Mindset – Choosing to think and communicate in a way that promotes positivity.

Learning How to Unlearn – The ability to let go of previous thoughts, concepts, and opinions that no longer serve future goals.

REFERENCES

Asch, S.E. (1951). *Effects of group pressure on the modification and distortion of judgments.*

Pittsburgh, PA: Carnegie Press.

Canfield, J. (2019). The success formula that puts you in control of your destiny. Retrieved

from https://www.jackcanfield.com/blog/ the-formula-that-puts-you-in-control-of-

success/.

Carter, K. (2018). The one that got away. Retrieved from www.espn.com/outdoors/fishing/news/

story?page=world_record_bass_dies.

Chang, R. (2014). How to make hard choices. Retrieved from https://www.ted.com/talks/

ruth_chang_how_to_make_hard_choices?language=en.

Comaford, C. (2013). Got inner peace? 5 ways to get it now. Retrieved from

https://www.forbes.com/sites/christinecomaford/2012/04/04/ got-inner-peace-5

-ways-to-get-it-now/#389d26776672.

Covey, S. R. (2004). *The 7 habits of highly effective people: restoring the character ethic.* New

York, NY: Free Press.

Csikszentmihalyi, M. (1997). *The masterminds series. Finding flow: the psychology of*

engagement with everyday life. New York, NY: Basic Books.

Dyer, W. W. (2010). Open your mind. Retrieved from https://www.drwaynedyer.com/blog/open-your-mind/.

Dyer, W.W. (2016). The wake (blaming the past). Retrieved from https://www.youtube.com/watch?v=jJFyWilWBE0.

Festinger, L. (1957). *A theory of cognitive dissonance.* Evanston, IL: Row, Peterson and Co.

Ford, V. (1974). No Woman, No Cry [Recorded by B. Marley and the Wailers]. On *Natty Dread*
[Vinyl]. Kingston, Jamaica: Harry J. Studios.

Godlasky, A., & Dastagir, A. E. (2018). Suicide rate up 33% in less than 20 years, yet funding
lags behind other top killers. Retrieved from https://www.usatoday.com/in-depth/
news/investigations/surviving-suicide/2018/11/28/
suicide-prevention-suicidal-thoughts-
research-funding/971336002.

Hartley, R. (2015). Why the best hire might not have the perfect resume Retrieved from
https://www.ted.com/talks/
regina_hartley_why_the_best_hire_might_not_have_the_
perfect_resume#t-94179.

Hyland, P., Lee, R., & Mills, M. (2015). Mindfulness at work: a new approach to improving
individual and organizational performance. *Industrial and Organizational Psychology,*
8(4), pp. 576-602. doi:10.1017/iop.2015.41.

Leytem, M. & Stark, E. (2016). The role of social influence on how residence hall inhabitants
respond to fire alarms. *The Journal of College and University Student Housing, 43(1),*
pp. 60-73.

Lippincott, M. (2018). Deconstructing the relationship between mindfulness and leader
effectiveness. *Leadership & Organization Development Journal,*
39(5), pp.650-664.
https://doi.org/10.1108/LODJ-11-2017-0340.

Mendoza-Denton, R. (2012). The spotlight effect. Retrieved from
https://www.psychologytoday.com/us/blog/
are-we-born-racist/201206/the-spotlight-

effect.

Mueller, P., & Oppenheimer, D.(2014). The pen is mightier than the keyboard: advantages of

longhand over laptop note taking. *Psychological Science, 25*(6), pp. 1159-1168.

http://journals.sagepub.com/doi/10.1177/0956797614524581.

Pickhartz, E. (2016). Rick Clunn becomes oldest bassmaster tournament winner at florida

elite event. Retrieved from www.wideopenspaces.com/ rick-clunn-becomes-oldest-

bass-tournament-winner-florida-elite-event/.

Recreational Fishing - Statistics & Facts. (2017). Retrieved from https://www.statista.com/topics/1163/recreational-fishing/.

Russell, S. (2014). Largemouth bass reproduction . Retrieved from http://www.bassfishingalabama.com/Reproduction.html.

Sherif, M. (1958). Superordinate goals in the reduction of inter-group conflict. *American Journal

of Sociology, 63,* pp. 349–356. https://doi.org/10.1086/222258.

Simonds, R. (Producer), & Davis, T. (Director). (1998). *Half Baked* [Motion picture]. United

States: Universal Pictures.

Spector,N. (2017). Smiling can trick your brain into happiness-and boost your

health. Retrieved from https://www.nbcnews.com/better/health/ smiling-can-trick-your-

brain-happiness-boost-your-health-ncna822591.

Vital Signs. (2019). Retrieved from https://my.clevelandclinic.org/health/articles/10881-vital-signs.

Vogel, E. A., Rose, J. P., Roberts, L. R., & Eckles, K. (2014). Social comparison, social media,

and self-esteem. Retrieved from https://www.researchgate.net/ publication/205507421_social_comparison_social_media_ and_self_esteem.

What is Root Cause Analysis (RCA)? (n.d.). Retrieved from
https://asq.org/quality-resources/root-cause-analysis.

Appendix

To the incredible people who dedicated their time and energy to this dream of mine...

Alisha Leytem	*Jason Jaber*
Wes Leytem	*Deborah Braun*
Austin Marshall	*Drew Brush*
Callie Leytem	*Richard Fursman*
Kelli Baxter	*Kristy Jungemann*
Drew Speight	*Sherine Kurian*
Chris Leytem	*Maraya Smith*
Lois Elswick	*Anna Ruemenapf*
Paul Fursman	*Dan Sachau*
Jake Forsman	*Christine Whelan*
Suzie Morgan Pahlke	*Alexcis Lopez*
Wayne Leytem	*Nancy Leytem*

From the bottom of my heart... Thank You!

Made in the USA
Las Vegas, NV
15 November 2020